Python Scrape for Links in Web

Discover Powerful Techniques to Gather and Organize Web Links Efficiently

Alex Hart

3

Discover other Books in the Series

5

Disclaimer

The information provided in *Python Scrape for Links in Web: Discover Powerful Techniques to Gather and Organize Web Links Efficiently* by Alex Hart is for **educational and informational purposes only**. This book is intended to help readers understand and implement web scraping techniques using Python in a lawful and responsible manner.

The techniques discussed in this book should be used only for ethical purposes, such as improving web applications, data gathering with consent, or securing online information. The author **does not endorse or condone any illegal activities**, including but not limited to unauthorized access to websites, scraping protected content without permission, or violating any data protection regulations.

Users are fully responsible for complying with the laws and regulations applicable in their jurisdiction, including the **Computer Fraud and Abuse Act** (CFAA), **General Data Protection Regulation** (GDPR), or any other relevant legal frameworks.

Introduction

Welcome to *"Python Scrape for Links in Web: Discover Powerful Techniques to Gather and Organize Web Links Efficiently"*—your gateway to mastering one of the most powerful skills in the modern digital world. Whether you're a **Python programmer**, a **web developer**, a **cybersecurity professional**, or an **ethical hacker**, this book will arm you with cutting-edge techniques to extract, organize, and utilize web links like never before.

Enter **web scraping**—a game-changer that empowers you to mine massive amounts of data with precision and speed. Throughout this book, you'll learn how to wield **Python's scraping libraries**, including **BeautifulSoup** and **Selenium**, to automate the extraction of valuable links from websites, filtering out noise and zeroing in on exactly what you need.

We'll explore **real-world use cases** from building web applications to ensuring cybersecurity, offering practical examples to sharpen your skills. Each chapter is crafted to not only teach you the mechanics of scraping but also to dive into the **security implications**, helping you stay on the ethical side of hacking while protecting your data and systems.

By the end of this book, you'll be equipped with a robust toolkit to harness the full potential of web scraping— making you more efficient, resourceful, and ahead of the curve in today's fast-paced tech environment. Whether you're looking to develop smarter web apps, protect sensitive information, or simply expand your Python expertise, this is your go-to resource.

Get ready to dive deep and uncover the powerful techniques that will transform how you gather and organize web data!

Chapter 1: Fundamentals of Web Scraping

Web scraping, the process of automatically extracting information from websites, has emerged as a vital skill for researchers, marketers, journalists, and many professionals across various domains. This chapter serves as an introduction to the fundamentals of web scraping, covering its basic concepts, tools, techniques, and ethical considerations.

What is Web Scraping?

Web scraping involves programmatically retrieving and parsing content from websites to transform unstructured data into a structured format. The data extracted can range from simple textual information to complex datasets involving images, videos, and other multimedia elements. The primary goal is to gather relevant data and analyze it for specific insights, trends, or applications.

Use Cases of Web Scraping

Web scraping has a plethora of applications that span across industries:

Market Research: Companies utilize web scraping to analyze competitors' pricing strategies, product offerings, and customer feedback.
Data Journalism: Journalists often scrape data from public sources to uncover trends or inconsistencies in reporting.

Lead Generation: Businesses scrape websites for potential client information to build marketing andsales databases.
Academic Research: Researchers gather data for studies, surveys, and various educational purposes.
Travel Aggregation: Websites like Google Flights or Kayak scrape data from various airlines and travel agencies to provide users with the best deals.

How Web Scraping Works

Web scraping typically involves several key steps:

Requesting a Web Page: The scraping process begins by sending an HTTP request to a target webpage. The server hosting the webpage responds with the page's HTML content. This can be done using libraries like `requests` in Python, which simplifies the process of interacting with web servers.

Parsing HTML Content: Once the HTML content is retrieved, the next step is to parse it. This involves identifying the data elements of interest within the HTML structure. Libraries like Beautiful Soup,lxml, or Scrapy in Python are commonly used for parsing and navigating the HTML tree structure.

Extracting Data: After parsing, the desired data (such as text, links, images, etc.) can be extracted bytargeting specific HTML tags, classes, or IDs where the data resides.

Storing the Data: The final step is to store the extracted data in a structured format that is easy to analyze. Common storage formats include CSV files, databases (like SQLite or MongoDB), or directly into data analytics tools.

A Simple Example

To illustrate the web scraping process, consider a simple example of scraping book titles from an online bookstore.

Send an HTTP request: Using a library like `requests`, you might use:
```python
import requests
url = "http://books.toscrape.com/"
response = requests.get(url)
```

Parse the HTML: With Beautiful Soup:
```python
from bs4 import BeautifulSoup
soup = BeautifulSoup(response.text, 'html.parser')
```

Extract Data:
```python
books = soup.find_all('h3')
titles = [book.find('a')['title'] for book in books]
```

Store Data: Finally, save the titles to a CSV file:
```python
import csv
with open('book_titles.csv', 'w', newline='') as file:
    writer = csv.writer(file)
    writer.writerow(["Title"])
    for title in titles: writer.writerow([title])
```

```

## Tools and Technologies

Web scraping can be accomplished using various programming languages and tools, but Python has become the most popular due to its simplicity and the effectiveness of its libraries. Some of the key tools and libraries include:

**Requests**: For sending HTTP requests and handling responses.
**Beautiful Soup**: For parsing HTML and XML documents.
**Scrapy**: A powerful web scraping framework that provides an efficient way to extract and manage data.
**Selenium**: A tool to automate web browsers, useful for scraping dynamic content loaded via JavaScript.
**Pandas**: For data analysis and manipulation, helping to clean and organize the scraped data. ## Ethical Considerations
While web scraping can provide valuable data, it is important to consider the ethical implications:

**Respect Robots.txt**: Before scraping a website, always check its `robots.txt` file, which indicates the pages that can and cannot be crawled by bots.

**Avoid Overloading Servers**: Make requests at a respectful rate to avoid impacting the website's performance. Using throttling or sleep functions between requests is a good practice.
```

Compliance with Terms of Service: Ensure compliance with the website's terms of service. Some sites explicitly prohibit scraping, and violating these terms could lead to legal issues.

Data Privacy: Be mindful of user data and privacy concerns, especially when scraping personal information.

Web scraping is a powerful technique for data extraction that has numerous applications across various fields. By understanding the core principles and ethical considerations, anyone can harness the potential of web scraping to derive insights and drive informed decisions. In the following chapters, we will delve into more advanced techniques, best practices, and real-world scenarios to strengthen your web scraping skills further.

The Power of Python for Web Scraping

Businesses seek insights, researchers gather knowledge, and developers create applications—all leading to a growing demand for web scraping. Among the myriad of languages suitable for this task, Python stands out as a versatile and powerful tool. This chapter delves into the reasons behind Python's prowess in web scraping, the libraries that simplify the process, and the ethical considerations that must accompany such endeavors.

The Rise of Python

Python's ascent in the programming community can be attributed to several factors: its simplicity, readability, and extensive community support. These traits make it an ideal choice for both novice and experienced developers. For web scraping, specifically, Python offers several libraries designed to facilitatethe extraction of data from websites, allowing developers to focus more on data analysis rather than the intricacies of network management or HTML parsing.

Why Python?

Ease of Use: Python's syntax is straightforward, allowing users to write and read code more comfortably than many other programming languages. This ease of use is especially beneficial for beginners who may be overwhelmed by the complexities of other languages.

Rich Ecosystem: Python's extensive collection of libraries is perhaps its most compelling feature. Libraries such as Beautiful Soup, Scrapy, and Requests allow developers to handle common tasks associatedwith web scraping efficiently.

Community Support: The Python community is vast and diverse. This means that when challenges arise, solutions are often just a search away, whether in the form of documentation, forums, or collaborativeprojects.

Libraries That Empower Web Scraping

Python's arsenal for web scraping is rich with libraries, each serving a unique purpose in the scraping process. Understanding these tools is crucial for harnessing the full potential of Python in web scrapingendeavors.

1. **Requests**

Requests is a simple yet powerful library for making HTTP requests. Its intuitive API allows users to send HTTP requests easily, handling complexities like URL encoding and session management transparently. When starting any web scraping project, it typically begins with fetching the web page's HTML source, andRequests serves this function flawlessly.

```python
import requests

url = 'http://example.com' response = requests.get(url)
html_content = response.text
```

2. **Beautiful Soup**

Once the HTML content is retrieved, Beautiful Soup comes into play. This library allows for easy navigationand manipulation of the parse tree of HTML and XML documents. With Beautiful Soup, developers can extract specific data points using simple, readable commands.

```python
from bs4 import BeautifulSoup

soup = BeautifulSoup(html_content, 'html.parser') title = soup.find('title').text
print(title)
```

3. **Scrapy**

For larger-scale scraping projects, Scrapy is a robust framework that handles both fetching and parsing data. It is designed for speed and efficiency, allowing developers to build powerful spiders that can scrape multiple pages and even follow links autonomously.

```python
import scrapy

class ExampleSpider(scrapy.Spider): name = 'example'
start_urls = ['http://example.com']

def parse(self, response):
title = response.css('title::text').get() yield {'title': title}
```

4. **Pandas**

While not strictly a web scraping tool, Pandas plays an integral role in the post-scraping process. This library excels at data manipulation and analysis, making it easier to convert scraped data into a format suitable for manipulation, visualization, or storage.

```python
import pandas as pd

data = {'Title': [title]}
df = pd.DataFrame(data)   df.to_csv('output.csv', index=False)
```

A Cautionary Note: Ethics and Legality

While the power of Python for web scraping is undeniable, it is essential to navigate these waters ethically and legally. Websites usually have terms of service that dictate how their data can be used. Scraping might violate these terms, potentially leading to your IP being banned or, in extreme cases, legal action.

Best Practices

Respect the Robots.txt File: Most websites include a `robots.txt` file that outlines permissions for web crawlers. Always check this file before scraping.

Throttle Your Requests: Avoid overwhelming the target server by spacing out your requests. This minimizes the strain on the website and reduces the chances of being blocked.

Identify Yourself: Use user-agent headers to identify your scripts responsibly. This can prevent your requests from being mistaken for unwanted bot traffic.

Consider Alternatives: APIs (Application Programming Interfaces) often provide a legitimate and structured way to access data. Check if the data you seek is available through an API before scraping.

By respecting site policies, adhering to legal guidelines, and applying best practices, developers can harness the full potential of Python to make the most of the data-rich environments of the internet. As we continue to explore the depths of web scraping, Python remains not just a language but a fundamental ally in the quest for knowledge and insight in the digital age.

Web link scraping with python basics

Whether for data analysis, research, or automation purposes, web scraping enables users to gather large amounts of data from various online sources efficiently. In this chapter, we will delve into the fundamental concepts of web scraping using Python, one of the most popular programming languages for this task.

What is Web Scraping?

Web scraping is the process of extracting data from websites. This technique can yield valuable insights by transforming unstructured web data into a structured format, such as CSV files or databases. Web scraping can be used in numerous applications, including market research, pricing analysis, and academic data collection.

Legal and Ethical Considerations

Before diving into the technical aspects, it is crucial to understand the legal and ethical implications of web scraping. Websites have terms of service that often prohibit automated data collection. Always review these terms, seek permission when necessary, and be mindful of robots.txt files, which indicate which parts of a website can or cannot be crawled by bots.

Setting Up Your Environment

To begin scraping, you will need to set up a Python environment. The two most popular libraries for web scraping in Python are `BeautifulSoup` and `Requests`. Here's how to get started:

Install Python: Ensure you have Python 3.x installed on your machine. You can download it from [python.org](https://www.python.org/downloads/).

Install the Required Libraries: Use pip, the Python package installer, to install the libraries:

```bash
pip install requests beautifulsoup4
```

Setting Up a New Project: Create a new directory for your web scraping project, and within that directory, create a new Python file (e.g., `scraper.py`).

Making Your First Request

Let's start with a simple example of how to send a request to a web page and retrieve its content using the `Requests` library. The following code snippet demonstrates how to do this:

```python
import requests
```

```python
# URL of the website we want to scrape url = 'https://example.com'

# Sending a GET request response = requests.get(url)

# Check the response status codeif response.status_code == 200:
print("Successfully retrieved the webpage")else:
print(f"Failed to retrieve the webpage. Status code: {response.status_code}")
```
```

In this code, we send a GET request to `https://example.com`. The status code 200 indicates success, whileother codes signal potential issues, such as 404 (not found) or 403 (forbidden).

## Parsing HTML Content

Once you have the HTML content of the web page, the next step is to parse it and extract the data you need. `BeautifulSoup` makes this process intuitive and user-friendly. Here's how to use it:

```python
from bs4 import BeautifulSoup

# Create a BeautifulSoup object and specify the parser
soup = BeautifulSoup(response.text, 'html.parser')

# Print the formatted HTML (for debugging purposes)
print(soup.prettify())
```
```

```
```

The `prettify()` function will output a nicely formatted version of the HTML, which can be useful for understanding the structure of the page.

Extracting Data

To extract specific elements from the HTML, you can use BeautifulSoup's search methods, such as `find()` and `find_all()`. Below is an example that demonstrates how to scrape all the links from a webpage:

```python
# Find all anchor tags (<a>)links = soup.find_all('a')

# Iterate through the found links and print the href attributefor link in links:
href = link.get('href')if href:
print(href)
```

In this example, we use `find_all('a')` to gather all anchor (`<a>`) tags, which typically contain hyperlinks.We then loop through these links and extract the value of the `href` attribute, which contains the URL.

Handling Relative URLs

Sometimes, the URLs found will be relative and may not work as standalone links. You can use the `urljoin` function from the `urllib.parse` module to convert relative URLs into absolute ones:

```python
from urllib.parse import urljoin

# Base URL for joining relative URLs base_url =
'https://example.com'

# Handle relative URLsfor link in links:
href = link.get('href')if href:
full_url = urljoin(base_url, href)print(full_url)
```

In this chapter, we have explored the fundamentals of web link scraping using Python. We learned how to send requests to web pages, parse HTML content, and extract valuable data, such as links. While this chaptercovers the basics, web scraping can be a complex task that sometimes requires dealing with JavaScript- rendered content, pagination, and data storage.

Chapter 2: Setting Up Your Python Environment

Whether you are a beginner or an experienced developer, understanding how to correctly set up your environment can save time and prevent frustration down the line. This chapter will guide you through the process of installing Python, setting up a virtual environment, and installing necessary packages and tools.

2.1 Installing Python

Before you can begin coding in Python, it must be installed on your system. Python is available for various operating systems including Windows, macOS, and Linux.

2.1.1 Downloading Python

Visit the Official Website: Go to the official Python website at[python.org](https://www.python.org).
Download the Installer: Click on the "Downloads" tab. The website should suggest the best version for your operating system (usually the latest stable release). Click the download link to get the installer.

2.1.2 Running the Installer

After downloading, locate the installer and follow these steps:

Windows: Double-click the `.exe` file to run it. Ensure you check the box that says **Add Python to

PATH** before clicking "Install Now." This simplifies running Python from the command line.
macOS: Open the downloaded `.pkg` file and follow the on-screen instructions. Python will be installed in `/usr/local/bin/python3`.
Linux: Many distributions already include Python. However, if you need to install it, use the package manager. For example, on Ubuntu, use the following command:
```bash
sudo apt update
sudo apt install python3
```

2.1.3 Verifying the Installation

To confirm Python is installed correctly, open a terminal or command prompt and run the followingcommand:
```bash
python --version
``` or
```bash
python3 --version
```

You should see the Python version number if it's installed correctly.## 2.2 Setting Up a Virtual Environment
To maintain a clean and organized workspace, it is best practice to use a virtual environment for yourprojects. A virtual environment is an isolated environment in which you can install packages without affecting the global Python installation.

2.2.1 Creating a Virtual Environment

Install `venv`: This module is included in the standard library for Python 3. If you are using Python 3.3 or newer, `venv` should already be available. If you're using Python 2.x, consider upgrading or use `virtualenv`.

Create the Environment: Navigate to the directory where you want to create your project and run the following command:
```bash
python -m venv myenv
```

Replace `myenv` with your desired environment name.

2.2.2 Activating the Virtual Environment
Windows:
```bash
myenv\Scripts\activate
```

macOS/Linux:
```bash
source myenv/bin/activate
```

Once activated, your command line will reflect the environment name, indicating that you're working within it.

2.2.3 Deactivating the Virtual Environment

To exit the virtual environment, simply run the command:
```bash
deactivate
```

This will return you to the global Python environment. ##

2.3 Installing Packages

Python's strength lies in its vast ecosystem of libraries and frameworks. The most common tool for package management is `pip`, which comes installed with Python.

2.3.1 Installing Packages with pip

While in your activated virtual environment, you can use `pip` to install packages easily:

```bash
pip install package_name
```

For example, to install a popular web framework called Flask, you would run:

```bash
pip install Flask
```

2.3.2 Keeping Track of Packages

As your project grows, you will likely install multiple libraries. To keep track of these, you can create a `requirements.txt` file, which lists all your project's dependencies. You can generate this file by running:

```bash
pip freeze > requirements.txt
```

Later, to install all the dependencies from this file in a new environment, use:

```bash
pip install -r requirements.txt
```

2.4 Code Editor Setup

Choosing a suitable code editor or Integrated Development Environment (IDE) is vital for coding productivity. Popular choices for Python include:

Visual Studio Code (VSCode): A lightweight editor with many extensions for Python development.
PyCharm: A powerful IDE specifically designed for Python with rich features.
Jupyter Notebook: Ideal for data science projects, allowing for interactive coding and visualization.

Each tool has its configuration options, but make sure to install Python extensions for better syntax highlighting, code linting, and debugging capabilities.

In this chapter, we walked through the essential steps to set up your Python environment. We discussed how to install Python, set up virtual environments to manage project-specific dependencies, install packages for various libraries, and select a code editor for efficient development.

Python Libraries for Web Scraping

With the proliferation of information available online, the

demand for web scraping has surged. Python, with its simplicity and rich ecosystem of libraries, has become the go-to programming language for web scraping tasks. In this chapter, we will explore some of the most popular Python libraries for web scraping, their features, and how to use them effectively.

1. Introduction to Web Scraping

Web scraping entails sending automated requests to websites, retrieving the HTML (i.e., the web page's source code), and then parsing or extracting relevant information from that code. This process can facilitate data collection for various purposes, such as data analysis, research, or creating datasets for machine learning. However, it is essential to respect the website's terms of service and legality regarding scraping practices.

2. Popular Python Libraries for Web Scraping ### 2.1 Requests
The **Requests** library is an essential package for making HTTP requests in Python. It simplifies the process of sending requests and handling responses. With Requests, acquiring the HTML content of a webpage becomes straightforward and user-friendly.

Installation:
```bash
pip install requests
```

Usage Example:
```python import requests
```

```python
url = 'https://example.com' response = requests.get(url)

if response.status_code == 200:
html_content = response.textelse:
print(f"Failed          to          retrieve          the          page:
{response.status_code}")
```

2.2 Beautiful Soup

Beautiful Soup is one of the most popular libraries for
parsing HTML and XML documents. It providesPythonic
idioms to navigate and search the parse tree, making it
easier to extract data from web pages.

Installation:
```bash
pip install beautifulsoup4
```

Usage Example:
```python
from bs4 import BeautifulSoup

soup = BeautifulSoup(html_content, 'html.parser')titles =
soup.find_all('h1')

for title in titles:
print(title.get_text())
```

2.3 Scrapy

30

Scrapy is an open-source and powerful web scraping framework designed for large-scale web scrapingprojects. It provides built-in support for handling requests, parsing responses, and even storing scraped data in various formats. Scrapy is perfect for projects that require speed and efficiency.

Installation:
```bash
pip install scrapy
```

Usage Example:
To create a new Scrapy project:
```bash
scrapy startproject myproject
```

Then, define a spider in `myproject/spiders/`. For instance:
```python
import scrapy

class MySpider(scrapy.Spider): name = 'my_spider'
start_urls = ['https://example.com']

def parse(self, response):
titles = response.css('h1::text').getall()for title in titles:
yield {'title': title}
```

You can run the spider with:
```bash
```

```
scrapy crawl my_spider -o output.json
```

2.4 Selenium

Selenium is a powerful tool for controlling web browsers programmatically. It is particularly useful for scraping dynamic websites that rely on JavaScript to load content. Selenium can interact with the web page as a human would, making it possible to click buttons, fill out forms, and navigate through elements that might be hidden or generated dynamically.

Installation:
```bash
pip install selenium
```

Usage Example:
```python
from selenium import webdriver

driver = webdriver.Chrome()
driver.get('https://example.com')
titles = driver.find_elements_by_tag_name('h1')for title in titles:
print(title.text)

driver.quit()
```

2.5 lxml

lxml is a high-performance library for parsing XML and HTML. It is particularly efficient for dealing with large documents and offers a simple and Pythonic way to interact with the data structures. It works seamlessly with XPath for selecting elements.

Installation:
```bash
pip install lxml
```

Usage Example:
```python
from lxml import html

tree = html.fromstring(html_content) titles = tree.xpath('//h1/text()')

for title in titles:
print(title)
```

3. Choosing the Right Library

The choice of the library often depends on the complexity of the scraping task at hand:

For simple scraping tasks on static web pages, **Requests** combined with **Beautiful Soup** is a reliable choice.
For large-scale scraping involving multiple pages and complex data extraction, **Scrapy** is highly recommended.

33

If you encounter dynamic content that requires user interaction, opt for **Selenium**.
For high-performance parsing of large documents, consider using **lxml**. ## 4. Best Practices for Web Scraping

When engaging in web scraping, you should adhere to the following best practices:

Respect Robots.txt: Always check the site's `robots.txt` file to understand what is permissible to scrape.
User-Agent Headers: Mimic legitimate browser requests by setting a User-Agent header.
Rate Limiting: Avoid overwhelming the server by introducing delays between requests.
Data Storage: Organize and store the extracted data in a consistent format (e.g., JSON, CSV, databases).
Error Handling: Implement robust error handling to manage failed requests and unexpected changes in website structure.

Python libraries facilitate various web scraping tasks, each with unique strengths and functionalities. By leveraging these libraries effectively, you can extract meaningful data from the vast ocean of information available online. However, always remember to scrape responsibly and ethically, keeping in mind the legal implications and site-specific rules. As you continue to explore and experiment with these libraries, your ability to extract and utilize data will only grow, paving the way for exciting new insights and opportunities.

Technique and precautions for web scraping with python

As industries increasingly rely on big data, Python has become the go-to programming language for developers and data analysts due to its robust libraries and simple syntax. However, while web scraping can provide tremendous benefits, it is crucial to understand the ethical and legal implications associated with it. This chapter will delve into the techniques for effectively scraping the web using Python, as well as the precautions you should take to avoid potential pitfalls.

4.1 Understanding Web Scraping

Web scraping refers to the automated process of extracting information from websites. It involves making requests to web pages and then parsing the HTML or XML content to gather specific data points. The collected data can range from textual information (such as news articles, product prices, or stock market data) to images or other multimedia content.

4.1.1 Common Libraries for Web Scraping

Requests: This library allows you to send HTTP requests easily. It handles the complexities ofconnecting to a web server and facilitates various HTTP operations (GET, POST, etc.).

Beautiful Soup: A library designed for web scraping

purposes to pull the data out of HTML and XML files by navigating the parse tree and searching for specific elements.

lxml: This library offers a fast and efficient way to parse HTML and XML, performing well for large documents.

Scrapy: A framework for web scraping that provides a comprehensive set of tools and features for scraping websites at scale, including handling cookies, sessions, and data storage.

Selenium: Often used for web scraping JavaScript-heavy websites, Selenium simulates a web browser and can interact with dynamic content that loads after the initial page render.

4.2 Techniques for Effective Web Scraping ### 4.2.1 Setting Up Your Environment
Before you start scraping, you need to set up your Python environment. Use `pip` to install the necessary libraries:

```bash
pip install requests beautifulsoup4 lxml scrapy selenium
```

4.2.2 Making HTTP Requests

Using the `Requests` library, you can start by making a simple HTTP GET request to retrieve a web page:

```python
import requests
```

```python
url = 'https://example.com' response = requests.get(url)

if response.status_code == 200:
print("Page retrieved successfully!")else:
print(f"Failed to retrieve page. Status code:
{response.status_code}")
```

4.2.3 Parsing HTML Content

Once you have the response, you can parse the HTML content with `Beautiful Soup`:

```python
from bs4 import BeautifulSoup

soup = BeautifulSoup(response.content, 'lxml') data = soup.find_all('div', class_='example-class') for item in data:
print(item.text)
```

4.2.4 Handling Pagination

Many websites present data over multiple pages, necessitating pagination handling. You can extract the URLfor the next page and repeat the request:

```python
next_page = soup.find('a', class_='next')['href'] while next_page:
response = requests.get(next_page)
```

```
soup = BeautifulSoup(response.content, 'lxml') # Process
the page...
next_page = soup.find('a', class_='next')
next_page = next_page['href'] if next_page else None
```

4.2.5 Managing Rate Limiting

To avoid overwhelming a server, incorporate delays
between your requests:

```python import time

for item in data:
print(item.text)
time.sleep(1) # Delay for 1 second
```

4.2.6 Using Proxies and User Agents

Some websites can block requests from automated scripts.
To mitigate this, use a variety of user agents and proxies:

```python
headers = {'User-Agent': 'Mozilla/5.0 (Windows NT 10.0;
Win64; x64) AppleWebKit/537.36 (KHTML, like Gecko)
Chrome/58.0.3029.110 Safari/537.3'}

response = requests.get(url, headers=headers)
```

4.2.7 Scraping JavaScript-Rendered Content For
websites loaded with JavaScript, use Selenium:

```
```

```python
from selenium import webdriver

driver = webdriver.Chrome()driver.get(url)
content = driver.page_source
soup = BeautifulSoup(content, 'lxml')
```

4.3 Precautions and Ethical Considerations ### 4.3.1 Legal Implications

Before scraping, it is essential to check the website's `robots.txt` file and review the terms of service to understand the permissible use of the site's content.

4.3.2 Rate Limiting and Throttling

To avoid getting your IP banned, ensure that you respect the site's rate limits. Excessive requests can lead to temporary or permanent blocking.

4.3.3 Data Privacy

Be mindful of the data you are collecting. Personal or sensitive data should not be scraped without proper consent and adherence to data protection regulations, such as GDPR.

4.3.4 Respecting Copyright

While scraping publicly available content is generally accepted, reusing scraped data, especially for commercial purposes, can infringe on copyright protection. Always give credit to the original source whenever applicable.

4.3.5 Error Handling

Incorporate robust error handling into your scripts to gracefully manage unexpected issues like broken links, timeouts, or incomplete data.

Web scraping with Python can be a powerful tool for data collection and analysis, providing insights into various domains. By employing the techniques detailed in this chapter and adhering to ethical practices, you can create efficient and respectful scraping scripts. As you advance in your web scraping journey, continue to seek out best practices and be vigilant about changes in website structures and policies that may affect your work.

Chapter 3: HTML and Web Structure Basics

The world of web development is expansive and constantly evolving. At the heart of this digital universe lies HTML, the backbone of web content. Understanding HTML and its role in web structure is fundamental for anyone aspiring to create websites or web applications. This chapter will guide you through the core concepts of HTML, its syntax, and how it contributes to the overall architecture of a webpage.

3.1 What is HTML?

HTML, or HyperText Markup Language, is the standard markup language used to create web pages. Developed in the early days of the internet, HTML provides a way to structure content and define how it will be displayed in web browsers. HTML is a cornerstone technology of the World Wide Web, often used alongside CSS (Cascading Style Sheets) and JavaScript to create dynamic, visually appealing, and interactive websites.

3.1.1 The Structure of HTML

At the most basic level, an HTML document consists of a series of elements marked by tags. These tags tell the browser how to display the content contained within them. An HTML document begins with a `<!DOCTYPE html>` declaration followed by an `<html>` element that wraps all the content on the page. Within the `<html>` tag, you will find two main sections:

the `<head>` and the `<body>`.

Head: The `<head>` section contains meta-information about the document, such as its title, character set, and links to stylesheets or scripts. This part of the document isn't visible to users but is crucial for defining how the page operates and appears.

Body: The `<body>` section includes the actual content that users see and interact with, such as text, images, videos, links, and other multimedia.

Example of a Basic HTML Document

Here is a simple example of an HTML document that incorporates the essential elements discussed:

```html
<!DOCTYPE html>
<html lang="en">
<head>
<meta charset="UTF-8">
<meta name="viewport" content="width=device-width, initial-scale=1.0">
<title>My First Web Page</title>
</head>
<body>
<h1>Welcome to My Website</h1>
<p>This is my first paragraph of text on my website. I am excited to learn HTML!</p>
<a href="https://www.example.com">Visit Example.com</a>
</body>
```

```
</html>
```

In this example, the document is structured clearly, allowing the browser to render a title in the tab and display a header, paragraph, and a link in the body.

3.2 HTML Elements and Tags

HTML documents are built using different types of elements, each defined by tags. Below, we will explore some of the most common HTML elements and their functions.

3.2.1 Headings

HTML provides six levels of headings, ranging from `<h1>` (the most important) to `<h6>` (the least important). Headings are crucial for organizing content and conveying structure to both users and search engines.

```html
<h1>Main Title</h1>
<h2>Subheading</h2>
<h3>Minor Heading</h3>
```

3.2.2 Paragraphs

Content is generally structured into paragraphs using the `<p>` tag. Paragraphs create readable blocks of text, making it easier for users to process information.

```html
<p>This is a paragraph of text. It can include multiple sentences and is a fundamental building block of HTML content.</p>
```

3.2.3 Links and Anchors

Links allow users to navigate between different pages or sections of a site. The `<a>` tag defines hyperlinks, where the `href` attribute specifies the URL.

```html
<a href="https://www.example.com">Click here to visit Example.com!</a>
```

3.2.4 Images

Images can enhance a webpage by providing visual context to the content. The `<img>` tag is used to embed images, using the `src` attribute to define the image's URL.

```html
<img src="image.jpg" alt="Description of the image" />
```

3.2.5 Lists

HTML supports both ordered (numbered) and unordered (bulleted) lists. These are created using the `<ol>` and `<ul>` tags, respectively, with individual list items marked with `<li>`.

```html
<ul>

<li>Item 1</li>
<li>Item 2</li>
<li>Item 3</li>
</ul>
```

3.3 HTML Attributes

Attributes provide additional information about elements. They are always included in the opening tag and generally come in name/value pairs, separated by equal signs. Common attributes include `id`, `class`, `style`, and `href`.

Example of Attributes

```html
<p id="introduction" class="text">This is an introductory paragraph.</p>
<a                    href="https://www.example.com" target="_blank">Open in a new tab</a>
```

In this example, the paragraph has an `id` attribute that uniquely identifies it and a `class` attribute that could be used for applying styles with CSS.

3.4 Semantic HTML

45

Semantic HTML refers to the use of HTML markup that conveys meaning about the content it contains. By using semantic elements, developers can provide additional context to both browsers and search engines, enhancing accessibility and SEO (Search Engine Optimization).

Examples of semantic elements include:

`<header>`: Defines a header for a document or section.
`<nav>`: Contains navigation links.
`<article>`: Represents a self-contained piece of content.
`<section>`: Defines a themed grouping of content.
`<footer>`: Defines a footer for a document or section.

Example of Semantic Structure

```html
<article>
<header>
<h2>Article Title</h2>
<p>Published on <time datetime="2023-01-01">January 1, 2023</time></p>
</header>
<p>This is the content of the article.</p>
<footer>
<p>Written by <a href="#">Author Name</a></p>
</footer>
</article>
```

Understanding the basics of HTML and web structure is essential for anyone venturing into web development. HTML provides the foundational building blocks for creating web pages, allowing developers to structure content coherently and accessibly. In this chapter, we've explored the essential elements of HTML, including its syntax, various tags, and the importance of semantic structure.

Understanding HTML Elements and Tags

HyperText Markup Language (HTML) is the backbone of web development. It is the standard language used to create and design web pages. Understanding HTML is essential for anyone seeking to build a website, as it provides the structure and meaning of content. In this chapter, we will explore HTML elements and tags, focusing on their definitions, roles, and practical applications.

What are HTML Elements?

An HTML element is a fundamental building block of a web page. It comprises two main parts: a start tag and an end tag, with content in between. For instance, in a simple paragraph element like this:

```html
<p>This is a paragraph.</p>
```

Start Tag: `<p>`
Content: `This is a paragraph.`
- **End Tag**: `</p>`

In this example, the `<p>` and `</p>` tags define a

47

paragraph element, and the text between them is the content that the paragraph displays on the web page.

Components of HTML Elements

Every HTML element has three primary components:

Start Tag: This indicates the beginning of an element. The start tag consists of the element's name enclosed in angle brackets. For example, `<h1>` is the start tag for a top-level heading.

Content: This is the text or other HTML elements that the start and end tags encapsulate. The content can be plain text, hyperlinks, images, lists, or even other HTML elements.

End Tag: This signifies the end of an element. It has the same name as the start tag but includes a forward slash before the element's name. For example, `</h1>` is the end tag for the heading element.

Understanding HTML Tags

HTML tags are the codes that represent HTML elements. They are essentially "instructions" for the web browser. HTML uses two types of tags: **paired tags** and **self-closing tags**.

Paired Tags

Paired tags, as seen in the previous paragraph example, consist of both a start and an end tag. Most HTML elements, such as paragraphs (`<p>`), headings (`<h1>` to `<h6>`), and divs (`<div>`), are paired.

Example:

```html
<div>
<h1>Welcome to My Website</h1>
<p>This is a simple website created to illustrate HTML elements.</p>

</div>
```

Self-Closing Tags

Self-closing tags do not have an end tag. They are used for elements that do not require any content between start and end tags. Examples include line breaks, images, and horizontal rules:

```html
<br>
<img src="image.jpg" alt="An example image">
<hr>
```

In the case of the `<img>` tag above, it denotes an image and includes attributes that define properties like the `src` (source) of the image and `alt` (alternative text) for accessibility.

Attributes: Enhancing HTML Elements

HTML tags can be enhanced with **attributes** that provide additional information about an element. Attributes are placed within the start tag and consist of a name and a value pair. For instance:

```html
<a                    href="https://www.example.com" target="_blank">Visit Example</a>
```

In this example:

The `<a>` tag defines a hyperlink.
The `href` attribute specifies the URL the link points to, and `target="_blank"` indicates that the link should open in a new tab.

Common HTML Attributes

class: Assigns a class name to the element for styling purposes.
id: A unique identifier for the element, used for styling and navigation.
style: Inline CSS styles that will apply to that specific element.
title: Provides additional information about the element, typically displayed as a tooltip on hover. ## Nesting HTML Elements
HTML elements can be nested, meaning that one element can contain another. This allows for the creation of complex layouts and structures. For instance:

```html
<div class="container">
<h1>Main Title</h1>
<p>This paragraph is part of the main content.</p>
<div>
<h2>Subheading</h2>
<p>More detailed information can go here.</p>
</div>
</div>
```

Here, we see that the `<div>` elements contain headings and paragraphs. Nesting elements allows for a more organized and manageable structure, which is essential for both design and SEO.

Understanding HTML elements and tags is crucial for anyone venturing into the realm of web development. As you've learned, elements form the basic structure of HTML documents, and tags serve as the syntax to create and manipulate these elements. By grasping the roles of paired and self-closing tags, as well as attributes, you gain the ability to craft web pages that are not only functional but also rich in content and design.

Navigating the DOM for Effective Link Extraction

Extracting links from a web page is a common task in web scraping and data processing. Links can guide research, serve as data points, or help automate navigation through various resources on the internet. This chapter will equip you with the tools and knowledge to efficiently navigate the DOM using Python, focusing on libraries such as BeautifulSoup and lxml that simplify the process of link extraction.

Understanding the DOM Structure

The DOM is a hierarchical tree structure representing the elements of a web page, such as text, images, and, importantly, hyperlinks. Each link element is embedded within anchor tags (`<a>`), which usually include important attributes like:

href: The URL the link points to.
title: A brief description of the link's purpose.
rel: The relationship between the current document and the linked document.

To navigate the DOM effectively, one must understand the structure of a typical HTML document. Here's a simplified example:

```html
<html>
<head>
<title>Sample Page</title>
</head>
<body>
<h1>Welcome to the Sample Page</h1>
<p>Check out these links:</p>
<a href="https://example.com">Example</a>
```

```
<a href="https://another-example.com" title="Another
Example">Another Example</a>
</body>
</html>
```

In this example, the two `<a>` tags represent hyperlinks.
Extracting their URLs will be our primary goal.## Setting
Up the Environment
Before diving into code, ensure you have Python installed
along with the necessary libraries. You can install
BeautifulSoup and Requests easily using pip:

```bash
pip install beautifulsoup4 requests lxml
```

BeautifulSoup: A library for parsing HTML and XML
documents.
Requests: A simple HTTP library for making requests
to web pages. ## Fetching a Web Page

To extract links, we first need to fetch the HTML content
of a web page. This is accomplished using the Requests
library:

```python
import requests

url = 'https://example.com' response = requests.get(url)

if response.status_code == 200:
html_content = response.textelse:
print("Failed to retrieve the web page.")
```

```
```

This code snippet checks the HTTP response status and fetches the content if the request is successful.## Parsing the HTML with BeautifulSoup
Once we have the HTML content, we can parse it with BeautifulSoup:

```python
from bs4 import BeautifulSoup

soup = BeautifulSoup(html_content, 'lxml')
```

Here, `lxml` is specified as the parser for faster parsing. ## Extracting Links
To extract all links from the parsed HTML, we'll leverage BeautifulSoup's powerful querying capabilities. We can find all anchor tags and then extract the URLs:

```python
links = soup.find_all('a')

for link in links:
href = link.get('href')
title = link.get('title', 'No Title') print(fTitle: {title}, URL: {href}')
```

The `find_all` method retrieves all `<a>` tags, and we can access their `href` attributes directly. It's also good practice to handle missing attributes, which is why we provide a default value for the title.

Handling Relative URLs

When working with links, you might encounter relative URLs. To convert these to absolute URLs, we can use `urljoin` from the `urllib.parse` module:

```python
from urllib.parse import urljoin
```

```
for link in links:
href = link.get('href') absolute_url = urljoin(url, href)title
= link.get('title', 'No Title')
print(f'Title: {title}, URL: {absolute_url}')
```

This ensures that we have fully qualified URLs, which are crucial for navigating the web effectively. ## Handling Link Redirections and Other Complexities
Web scraping can sometimes involve more complex behavior, like redirections or JavaScript-generated content that requires additional tools. Libraries such as Selenium can help in these cases. Selenium allowsyou to control a web browser and interact with websites as an actual user would.

Advanced Techniques### Filtering Links
You might not always want to extract every link on the page. Filtering based on certain criteria, such as specific domains or keywords, can refine your extraction process:

```python
filtered_links = [link for link in links if 'example' in link.get('href', '')]
```

Rate Limiting and Best Practices

Web scraping should always be done responsibly. Implementing delays between requests can prevent overwhelming the server and reduce the risk of getting banned. The `time` library can be used to introduce pauses:

```python
import time

# Delay before the next request
time.sleep(2)
```

Navigating the DOM for effective link extraction using Python is an essential skill for anyone looking to gather data from the web. With libraries like BeautifulSoup and Requests, this task becomes straightforward. By understanding the structure of HTML documents and honing your skills in querying the DOM, you can efficiently extract valuable information that can serve various research and automation purposes.

Chapter 4: Using Beautiful Soup for Basic Link Scraping

Beautiful Soup, a powerful Python library, allows us to parse HTML and XML documents easily, making it an excellent choice for basic link scraping tasks. This chapter will guide you through the fundamental steps of using Beautiful Soup to scrape links from a webpage, providing practical examples along the way.

4.1 Understanding Beautiful Soup

Beautiful Soup simplifies the process of navigating, searching, and modifying the parse tree of an HTML or XML document. It provides Pythonic idioms for iterating, searching, and filtering data, effectively transforming complicated markup into easily navigable objects.

Before diving into the coding section, you will need to ensure you have the necessary libraries installed. You can install Beautiful Soup and the requests library, which is typically used to retrieve the content of webpages, by running the following command:

```bash
pip install beautifulsoup4 requests
```

4.2 Fetching the Webpage

The first step in scraping links is to fetch the webpage you want to scrape. You can use the `requests` library to make a simple GET request. Here's a snippet of code that demonstrates how to accomplish this:

```python
import requests

url = "http://example.com" response = requests.get(url)

# Check if the request was successful if response.status_code == 200:
print("Successfully fetched the webpage!")
webpage_content = response.text
else:
print("Failed to retrieve the webpage:", response.status_code)
```

In this code, we specify the URL of the webpage we want to scrape, make a GET request to that URL, and check if the request was successful by examining the status code.

4.3 Parsing the HTML

Once you have the HTML content of the webpage, the next step is to parse it using Beautiful Soup. The following code snippet demonstrates how to create a Beautiful Soup object:

```python
from bs4 import BeautifulSoup

soup = BeautifulSoup(webpage_content, 'html.parser')
```

In this example, we initialize a Beautiful Soup object with the HTML content we retrieved. The second argument, `'html.parser'`, specifies the parser we want to use. Beautiful Soup supports several parsers, but the built-in HTML parser is typically sufficient for most scraping tasks.

4.4 Finding Links in the HTML

With the Beautiful Soup object created, we can start extracting links from the webpage. Links in HTML are defined by the `<a>` tag, which usually contains an `href` attribute that specifies the URL of the link. To find all the links on the webpage, you can use the `find_all` method:

```python
# Find all anchor tags in the HTML links = soup.find_all('a')

# Extract the href attribute from each linkfor link in links:
href = link.get('href')if href:
print(href)
```

In this loop, we call `soup.find_all('a')` to retrieve all the anchor tags present in the document. We then iterate through each link, extracting the value of the `href` attribute, and printing it to the console. The conditional `if href:` ensures that we only print valid links.

4.5 Filtering Links

Not all links retrieved are necessarily useful for every application. You may want to filter the links to include only those that satisfy specific criteria—like only those that point to HTTPS URLs or contain certain keywords.

Here's an example that filters links starting with "https":

```python
https_links = [link.get('href') for link in links if link.get('href') and link.get('href').startswith('https')]
print("Filtered HTTPS links:")
for link in https_links:
print(link)
```

In this code, we use a list comprehension to create a new list containing only the links that start with "https".This way, we ensure that the printed links are secure.

4.6 Handling Relative Links

When scraping links, it's essential to recognize that some URLs may be relative paths rather than absoluteURLs. To handle relative links correctly, use the `urljoin` method from the `urllib.parse` module. Here's how you can adjust the previous code to handle both absolute and relative links:

```python
from urllib.parse import urljoin

absolute_links = []for link in links:
href = link.get('href')if href:
```

```
full_url          =          urljoin(url,          href)
absolute_links.append(full_url)

print("Absolute links:") for link in absolute_links:
print(link)
```

By using `urljoin`, we can convert relative links to absolute URLs based on the base URL of the page we are scraping.

In this chapter, we've learned how to use Beautiful Soup for basic link scraping. We covered how to fetch a webpage, parse its HTML content, extract links, filter them based on criteria, and handle relative URLs.
With these techniques under your belt, you're now equipped to begin scraping links from various websites.

Installing and Using Beautiful Soup

It provides Pythonic idioms for iterating, searching, and modifying the parse tree, making it an invaluable tool for web scraping, data mining, and web development. In this chapter, we'll explore the steps to install Beautiful Soup, and walk through its basic functionalities to get you started on your journey to extract data from web pages.

1. Introduction to Beautiful Soup

Beautiful Soup simplifies the task of parsing complicated HTML and XML documents. It transforms these documents into a tree structure, allowing easy data extraction and manipulation. Whether you are looking to pull specific content from a webpage or aggregate data, Beautiful Soup provides a straightforward interface to interact with the data.

2. Installing Beautiful Soup### 2.1 Pre-requisites
Before installing Beautiful Soup, you need to have Python installed on your computer. Beautiful Soup is compatible with Python 3.6 and later versions. You can download Python from the official website [python.org](https://www.python.org/downloads/) and follow the installation instructions for your platform (Windows, macOS, or Linux).

2.2 Using pip to Install Beautiful Soup

The simplest way to install Beautiful Soup is through pip, Python's package manager. To check if pip is installed, you can run the following command in your terminal or command prompt:

```bash
pip --version
```

If pip is not installed, you may need to install it first. For most Python installations, pip will already be available.

To install Beautiful Soup, run the following command in the terminal:

```bash
pip install beautifulsoup4
```

This command installs the latest version of Beautiful Soup, which can be imported and used in your Python scripts. Additionally, you'll often need a parser to work effectively with Beautiful Soup. The built-in `html.parser` works well, but you can also opt for `lxml` or `html5lib` for more complex parsing. You can install these libraries with:

```bash
pip install lxml html5lib
```

2.3 Verifying the Installation

To ensure that Beautiful Soup is installed correctly, you can check its version by starting a Python shell and running the following commands:

```python
from bs4 import BeautifulSoup print(BeautifulSoup.version_)
```

If the version number is displayed without errors, you have successfully installed Beautiful Soup. ## 3. Basic Usage of Beautiful Soup
Now that we have installed Beautiful Soup, let's discuss how to use it effectively. We'll cover how to create a Beautiful Soup object, navigate the parse tree, search for data, and modify the content.

3.1 Creating a Beautiful Soup Object

The first step in using Beautiful Soup is to create a Beautiful Soup object by passing in the HTML content of a webpage. For this example, we'll use a simple HTML string.

```python
``python html_doc = """
<html>
<head>
<title>The Dormouse's story</title>
</head>
<body>
<h1>Welcome to Beautiful Soup</h1>
<p class="title"><b>The Dormouse's story</b></p>
<p class="story">Once upon a time there were three little sisters; and their names were Elsie, Lacie and Tillie; and they lived at the bottom of a well.</p>
<p class="story">...</p>
</body>
</html>"""

soup = BeautifulSoup(html_doc, 'html.parser')
``
```

3.2 Navigating the Parse Tree

After you have created the Beautiful Soup object, you can navigate its elements:

```python
``python
# Accessing the title elementtitle = soup.title
print(title) # <title>The Dormouse's story</title>
```

65

```python
# Getting the text inside the title element
print(title.string) # The Dormouse's story

# Finding the first <h1> tagh1_tag = soup.find('h1')

print(h1_tag.string) # Welcome to Beautiful Soup
```

3.3 Searching the Parse Tree

Beautiful Soup provides several methods to search through the tree. Here are a few of the most commonly used:

`find()`: to find the first tag that matches a given filter.
`find_all()`: to find all tags that match a filter.
`select()`: to select elements based on CSS selectors.

```python
# Finding all <p> tags p_tags = soup.find_all('p')for p in p_tags:
print(p.string)
```

3.4 Modifying the Parse Tree

You can also modify the content of the parsed elements.

```python
# Modifying the text of the first <p> tag soup.p.string =
"This is a modified paragraph."
print(soup.p) # <p class="title"><b>This is a modified
paragraph.</b></p>
```

```
```

3.5 Extracting Data

Data extraction is one of the primary use cases for Beautiful Soup. You can use it to extract the required data for storage, analysis, or further processing.

```python
# Extracting text and classes from all paragraphs for p in soup.find_all('p'):
print(p.get_text(), p.get('class'))
```

Beautiful Soup is a versatile and easy-to-use library for parsing HTML and XML documents. Through this chapter, we learned how to install Beautiful Soup, create Beautiful Soup objects, and navigate, search, and modify the parse tree. In subsequent chapters, we will delve deeper into advanced features, error handling, and practical applications for web scraping using Beautiful Soup

Extracting Links from Web Pages with Beautiful Soup

Among the many tasks that a data scientist or a web developer may encounter, extracting hyperlinks from web pages serves not only as a foundational skill but also as an essential precursor to complex data scraping and mining operations. In this chapter, we will explore the powerful

Python library Beautiful Soup, which simplifies the process of parsing HTML and XML documents. Specifically, we will focus on how to extract links, a common requirement for various applications such as data collection, site analysis, and content aggregation.

What is Beautiful Soup?

Beautiful Soup is a Python library that makes it easy to scrape information from web pages. It creates parse trees from page source code, allowing users to navigate the parse tree and retrieve desired data. The library is particularly useful for handling the complexities of HTML and XML documents, which can often be messy or poorly structured.

To get started with Beautiful Soup, you will first need to ensure that you have the library installed. You can easily install Beautiful Soup using pip:

```bash
pip install beautifulsoup4 requests
```

Here, we will also install `requests`, another essential library for making HTTP requests to fetch the content of web pages.

Fetching HTML Content

Before we can extract links, we need to retrieve the HTML content of a webpage. This is where the `requests` library comes in handy. Here's how to fetch the

HTML content of a sample webpage:

```python
import requests

url = "https://example.com"
response = requests.get(url)

# Check if the request was successful
if response.status_code == 200:
    html_content = response.text
else:
    print(f"Failed to retrieve content: {response.status_code}")
```

In this example, we send a GET request to the web server and store the response. If the request is successful (HTTP status 200), we proceed to extract links from `html_content`.

Parsing the HTML

With the HTML content in hand, we can now parse it using Beautiful Soup. This involves creating a Beautiful Soup object from the HTML string:

```python
from bs4 import BeautifulSoup

soup = BeautifulSoup(html_content, 'html.parser')
```

The argument `'html.parser'` indicates that we want to use Python's built-in HTML parser. Beautiful Soup also supports other parsers, like `lxml`, which you can install

69

and use for additional performance if needed.

Extracting Links

To find all the hyperlinks (anchor tags `<a>`) on the page and extract their `href` attributes, you can use the `.find_all()` method. Here's how:

```python
# Find all anchor tags anchors = soup.find_all('a')

# Extract and print the URLslinks = []
for anchor in anchors:
href = anchor.get('href')
if href:  # Check if the href attribute exists
links.append(href)

# Display extracted linksfor link in links:
print(link)
```

In this snippet, we loop through each anchor tag found on the page. We use the `get()` method to safelyretrieve the `href` attribute, ensuring that we only append valid links to our list.

Handling Relative Links

Web pages often contain relative links, which means that some URLs do not contain the complete address (e.g., `/about`, rather than `https://example.com/about`). To convert relative URLs into absolute URLs, youcan utilize the `urljoin` function from Python's standard library:

```python
from urllib.parse import urljoin

absolute_links = []for link in links:
absolute_link        =        urljoin(url,        link)
absolute_links.append(absolute_link)

# Display absolute links
for abs_link in absolute_links:print(abs_link)
```

Here, `urljoin()` helps to create a full URL based on the base URL and the relative path, making it easier to navigate the web.

Dealing with Duplicates

In many scenarios, you might encounter duplicate links on the same page. To ensure that you get a uniquelist of links, you can convert your list of links to a set and then back to a list:

```python
unique_links = list(set(absolute_links))

# Display unique links
for unique_link in unique_links:
print(unique_link)
```

In this chapter, we have explored the fundamental steps involved in extracting links from web pages usingBeautiful

Soup. From fetching the HTML content to parsing it and extracting links in various formats—working with Beautiful Soup allows you to handle web data extraction efficiently.

As you dive deeper into the world of web scraping, you'll find that this foundational skill can be applied in various domains, ranging from SEO analysis to competitive research. Practice these techniques, experiment with different web pages, and enhance your data extraction capabilities.

Chapter 5: Advanced Link Scraping with Beautiful Soup

With tools like Beautiful Soup, you can efficiently navigate complex HTML structures to find the exact linksyou need. This chapter will delve into advanced techniques for link scraping using Beautiful Soup, enabling you to build more sophisticated and powerful web crawlers.

5.1 Understanding HTML Structure

Before we dive into scraping, it's crucial to have a foundational understanding of HTML. Web pages are structured as a hierarchy of elements, each identified by tags such as `<a>`, `<div>`, `<span>`, etc. The `<a>` tag is specifically used for hyperlinks, and its `href` attribute contains the URL of the link.### 5.1.1 Inspecting Web Pages
To effectively scrape links, you should inspect the web pages you'll be working with. Most modern browsersallow you to do this using developer tools. Right-click on a webpage and select "Inspect" (or press F12) to view the HTML structure. Familiarize yourself with the elements you want to extract, noting the parent elements and surrounding tags that may contain valuable information.

5.2 Setting Up Beautiful Soup

To get started with web scraping using Beautiful Soup, you need to have the library installed. If you haven't done so yet, you can install it via pip:

```bash
pip install beautifulsoup4 requests
```

5.2.1 Importing Libraries

Once installed, you can import the necessary libraries in your Python script:

```python
import requests
from bs4 import BeautifulSoup
```

5.2.2 Fetching the HTML Content

You can fetch the HTML content of a webpage using the `requests` library. For example:

```python
url = 'https://example.com' response = requests.get(url)

if response.status_code == 200:
html_content = response.textelse:
print(f"Failed to retrieve content: {response.status_code}")
```

```
```

5.3 Parsing HTML with Beautiful Soup

With the HTML content in hand, you can then parse it with Beautiful Soup:

```python
soup = BeautifulSoup(html_content, 'html.parser')
```

The parser allows you to navigate the HTML structure and extract the data you need.## 5.4 Extracting Links
Now, let's delve into the techniques for extracting links more effectively. Beautiful Soup provides various methods to locate elements, allowing you to adapt your scraping strategy to different structures.

5.4.1 Finding All Links

To find all the links on a page, you can use the `find_all()` method:

```python
links = soup.find_all('a')

for link in links:
href = link.get('href')print(href)
```

This code snippet retrieves all the `<a>` tags and prints their `href` attributes.### 5.4.2 Filtering Links
Often, you may want to filter links based on specific

attributes or text. For example, if you only want links that contain a certain keyword, you can do something like this:

```python
filtered_links = soup.find_all('a', href=lambda x: x and 'keyword' in x)

for link in filtered_links:
print(link.get('href'))
```

This highlights the power of lambda functions in filtering your results dynamically. ### 5.4.3 Navigating the Tree Structure
Beautiful Soup allows you to traverse the HTML tree structure, which can be especially useful when links are nested inside other tags. For example, if you want to extract links from a specific section of the webpage:

```python
section = soup.find('div', class_='specific-section')
links_in_section = section.find_all('a')
```

```
for link in links_in_section:
print(link.get('href'))
```

In this example, only links within a specified `div` are retrieved, giving you more control over what is scraped.

5.5 Handling Relative URLs

In many cases, the links you extract may be relative URLs (e.g., `/about`, `../contact`). To convert these into absolute URLs, you can use the `urljoin` function from the `urllib.parse` module:

```python
from urllib.parse import urljoin

base_url = 'https://example.com'for link in links:
relative_url = link.get('href')
absolute_url    =    urljoin(base_url,    relative_url)
print(absolute_url)
```

By joining the base URL with relative URLs, you ensure that you have full, navigable links. ## 5.6 Dealing with Redirects and Broken Links
When scraping, it's common to encounter redirects and broken links. To handle these gracefully, you can check the status of each link using another request:

```python
for link in links:
url = link.get('href')try:
```

```
r    =    requests.head(url,    allow_redirects=True)    if
r.status_code == 200:
print(f"Valid link: {url}")else:
print(f"Broken link: {url} - Status Code: {r.status_code}")
except Exception as e:
print(f"Error accessing {url}: {e}")
```

This proactive approach ensures that your application remains robust against changes in the web structure.## 5.7 Ethics and Best Practices in Web Scraping
As with any technology, ethical considerations are essential. Always:

Review the website's `robots.txt` file for scraping permissions.
Be respectful of the website's load; don't overwhelm it with rapid requests.
Consider using a delay between requests, especially when scraping large volumes.Here is an example with a delay:

```python
import time

for link in links:
time.sleep(1) # Wait for 1 second before the next request #
Process link
```

In this chapter, we explored various advanced techniques for scraping links using Beautiful Soup. By understanding HTML structure, filtering links, navigating the DOM tree, handling relative URLs, and respecting ethical considerations, you can build powerful web scraping applications. With these skills under your belt, you are well-equipped to tackle the next challenges in web scraping and data extraction, paving the way for deep data analysis and insights.

Handling Nested Tags and Complex Web Pages with Python

As web pages become more intricate, with dynamic content generated by JavaScript or nested structures, the challenges to extract meaningful information intensify. This chapter will explore methodologies and practical techniques to address these challenges using Python, focusing primarily on libraries such as BeautifulSoup and lxml.

Understanding HTML Structure

Before diving into extracting data from complex web pages, it's essential to have a clear understanding of HTML structure. HTML is essentially a tree of elements, where each tag can contain other tags, making it hierarchical. For example:

```html
<div>
<h1>Title</h1>
<p>This is a <strong>nested</strong> paragraph.</p>
<ul>
<li>Item 1</li>
<li>Item 2
<ul>
```

```
<li>Sub-item 1</li>
<li>Sub-item 2</li>
</ul>
</li>
</ul>
</div>
```

In this example, we have a `div` element containing nested `h1`, `p`, and `ul` tags. Understanding how to traverse this tree structure is fundamental when scraping data from nested HTML.

Setting Up Your Environment

Before we begin extracting data, ensure you have the necessary packages installed. You can install BeautifulSoup and requests using pip:

```bash
pip install beautifulsoup4 requests
```

Fetching Web Pages

To start scraping, we first need to retrieve the HTML content of the target web page. This can typically be accomplished using the `requests` library. For example:

```python
import requests

url = 'https://example.com' response = requests.get(url)
```

```python
if response.status_code == 200:
    html_content = response.textelse:
    print(f"Failed to retrieve webpage: {response.status_code}")
```

Parsing HTML with BeautifulSoup

Once we have the HTML content, we can utilize BeautifulSoup to parse the document. BeautifulSoup creates a parse tree from the page source, allowing for easy navigation and extraction of data.

```python
from bs4 import BeautifulSoup

soup = BeautifulSoup(html_content, 'html.parser')
```

Navigating Nested Tags

Navigating through nested tags can be achieved using various BeautifulSoup methods such as `find()`, `find_all()`, `select()`, and dot notation. Here are a few examples:

Finding the Title:
To extract the title from the nested `h1` tag:
```python
title = soup.find('h1').textprint("Title:", title)
```

Extracting Nested Paragraphs:

To extract the text from the paragraph which contains a nested strong tag:
```python
paragraph = soup.find('p').text print("Paragraph:", paragraph)
```

Iterating Over Nested Lists:
Suppose we want to extract all items from a nested list:
```python
items = soup.find_all('li')for item in items:
print("List item:", item.text)
```

Using CSS Selectors for Complex Structures

For complex web pages where elements might be deeply nested or styled with specific classes or IDs, CSSselectors provide a powerful means of accessing these elements.

```python
# Extract sub-items using CSS selectors

sub_items = soup.select('ul > li > ul > li')for sub_item in sub_items:
print("Sub-item:", sub_item.text)
```

Handling Dynamic Content with Selenium

Static scraping, as demonstrated above, may not suffice for web pages that dynamically load content using JavaScript. In such cases, initializing a browser instance

82

with Selenium can be beneficial.

First, install Selenium:

```bash
pip install selenium
```

Then set up a basic scraping function to fetch dynamic content:

```python
from selenium import webdriver
from selenium.webdriver.common.by import By import
time

# Initialize the WebDriver (make sure to specify the path
to your webdriver) driver =
webdriver.Chrome(executable_path='path/to/chromedriver') driver.get('https://example.com')

# Wait for resources to loadtime.sleep(3)

# Fetch page content after JavaScript execution
html_content = driver.page_source
soup = BeautifulSoup(html_content, 'html.parser')

# Extract data as beforedriver.quit()
```

Handling nested tags and complex web pages requires a solid understanding of HTML structure, effective use of libraries such as BeautifulSoup and Selenium, and sometimes a bit of creativity. By mastering these techniques, you can efficiently extract data from even the most convoluted web pages, unlocking a wealth of information for your applications and analyses.

Managing Multiple Web Page Structures with Dynamic
Parsing in Python

As the web is increasingly composed of disparate and often complex structures, the ability to manage and parse multiple web page layouts dynamically has become essential for data scientists, analysts, and developers alike. This chapter delves into the advanced strategies for managing multiple web page structures through the utilization of dynamic parsing techniques in Python.

The Need for Dynamic Parsing

Web pages can vary significantly in their layout and structure, especially when they are generated by different frameworks, content management systems, or even varying HTML standards. Static parsing methods often fall short due to:

Inconsistent HTML Structures: Unlike a single predefined schema, websites may implement varying tag hierarchies and attributes.
Dynamic Content Loading: Some websites utilize JavaScript to load content dynamically, meaning the desired data may not be immediately present in the initial HTML response.
Frequent UI Changes: Web pages are often updated with new layouts, which can break hard-coded scraping logic.

To overcome these challenges, dynamic parsing

techniques allow the creation of adaptable scraping scripts that can handle various page structures seamlessly.

Getting Started with Parsing in Python

Before diving into dynamic parsing, it's essential to set up your Python environment with the necessary libraries. Key libraries include:

Requests: For sending HTTP requests to fetch web pages.
Beautiful Soup: For parsing HTML and XML documents and navigating the parse tree.
lxml: An alternative parsing library that provides faster parsing capabilities.
Selenium: For handling dynamic content loading, as it can interact with JavaScript-heavy pages.
Pandas: For data manipulation and analysis once the data has been scraped. You can install these libraries using pip:
```bash
pip install requests beautifulsoup4 lxml selenium pandas
```

Dynamic Parsing Techniques

1. Building a Flexible Parsing Function

The first step in managing multiple web page structures is creating a flexible parsing function. This function should accept parameters that allow it to adapt to varying structures.

```python
from bs4 import BeautifulSoup

import requests

def dynamic_parse(url, structure=None):
response = requests.get(url)
soup = BeautifulSoup(response.content, 'html.parser')

if structure is None:
structure = detect_structure(soup) # Custom function to
identify the parse structure

data = extract_data(soup, structure)return data
```

2. Detecting Web Page Structures

To robustly handle varied structures, implement a
`detect_structure` function that analyzes the web page
and identifies key elements based on their attributes,
classes, or tags.

```python
def detect_structure(soup):
# Example logic to determine structureif soup.find('div',
class_='product'):
return 'product_page'
elif soup.find('table', class_='data'):return 'data_table'
else:
return 'default_structure'
```

3. Extracting Data Based on Structure

For each detected structure, create a specific extraction strategy. This might involve using different CSSselectors or XPath queries.

```python
def extract_data(soup, structure):
if structure == 'product_page': products = []
for item in soup.find_all('div', class_='product'): title = item.find('h2').text
price      =     item.find('span',      class_='price').text
products.append({'title': title, 'price': price})
return products
elif structure == 'data_table': table_data = []
rows = soup.find_all('tr') for row in rows:
cols = row.find_all('td') table_data.append([col.text for col in cols])
return table_data else:
return [] # Handles unknown structure
```

4. Handling Dynamic Content with Selenium

For pages that rely heavily on JavaScript to display content, Selenium can interact with the page as a real user would. Here's a simple example of using Selenium to get a page element dynamically:

```python
from selenium import webdriver

def dynamic_parse_with_selenium(url):
    driver = webdriver.Chrome()  # Ensure you have the ChromeDriver installeddriver.get(url)

    # Wait for content to loaddriver.implicitly_wait(10)

    page_source = driver.page_source
    soup = BeautifulSoup(page_source, 'html.parser')

    data = extract_data(soup, 'dynamic_structure')  # Assuming a known structuredriver.quit()
    return data
```

5. Data Storage and Utilization

Once the data is extracted, you may want to store it in a structured format for later analysis. Utilizing Pandas, you can convert your list of dictionaries into a DataFrame and save it to a CSV or database.

```python
import pandas as pd
```

```
def save_data_to_csv(data, filename='output.csv'):
df     =     pd.DataFrame(data)     df.to_csv(filename,
index=False)
```

Dynamic parsing is a powerful technique in any web scraping toolkit. By effectively managing multiple web page structures, Python developers can harness vast quantities of data from the web, regardless of how varied or complex site designs may be.

Chapter 6: Introduction A Web Scraping Framework

From research articles to social media posts, data is generated in abundance every minute. However, much of this information is unstructured and resides on various webpages, making it challenging to extract and utilize. This is where web scraping comes into play—a technique that allows us to programmatically gather data from the web.

Web scraping involves the automated extraction of information from websites. It can be as simple as retrieving a few data points from a single page or as complex as collecting vast datasets from multiple sites over time. The power and versatility of web scraping make it an invaluable tool for data analysts, researchers, marketers, and developers looking to leverage the wealth of information available online.

6.2 The Need for a Web Scraping Framework

Despite the convenience of web scraping, the process can be intricate and error-prone. Web pages are designed for human interaction, not automated data extraction. As such, web scraping often encounters challenges such as:

Dynamic Content: Many modern websites use JavaScript to load content dynamically, which can complicate direct data extraction.
Rate Limiting: Websites typically implement measures to prevent excessive requests from a single

source, which can lead to IP blocking and access issues.

Data Cleaning: Scraped data often requires substantial cleaning and transformation before it can be utilized effectively.

Robustness: Websites frequently change their layout and structure, causing scraping scripts to fail unexpectedly.

Given these challenges, using a well-structured web scraping framework is vital for streamlining the process, improving efficiency, and ensuring scalability.

6.3 Features of a Good Web Scraping Framework

A robust web scraping framework should encompass several key features:

Ease of Use: A user-friendly interface and clear documentation are essential for both novice and experienced developers to quickly get started.

Modularity: The ability to break down scraping tasks into reusable components allows developers to build more complex scraping solutions easily.

Error Handling: Comprehensive error handling mechanisms should be in place to deal with potential issues such as connection timeouts, data format changes, or captchas.

Concurrency Support: The framework should enable concurrent scraping to accelerate the data collection process without overwhelming the target website.

Data Storage Solutions: Built-in options for storing scraped data—such as support for databases, CSV files, or cloud storage—are crucial for managing extracted information.

Respectful Scraping: Incorporating features that encourage ethical scraping practices, such as adherence to `robots.txt` directives and rate limiting, is essential to prevent abuse.

6.4 Popular Web Scraping Frameworks

Several frameworks have emerged in the web scraping landscape, each with its own strengths and weaknesses. Here, we introduce a few notable ones:

Scrapy: One of the most powerful open-source frameworks for web scraping, Scrapy is built on Python and offers a comprehensive set of tools for extracting, processing, and storing data. Its asynchronous capabilities allow for fast and efficient scraping of large volumes of data.

Beautiful Soup: A Python library that provides simple methods for navigating and searching through the parse tree of HTML and XML documents. While not a complete framework, it is often used in conjunction with requests to scrape data from websites easily.

Puppeteer: Developed by Google, Puppeteer is a Node.js library that allows control of headless Chrome browsers. Ideal for scraping dynamic content, Puppeteer can handle JavaScript-heavy websiteseffortlessly.

Selenium: Originally designed for automating web applications for testing purposes, Selenium can also be used for web scraping. It supports multiple browsers and offers powerful capabilities for scrapingdynamic content, although it may require more resources than simpler libraries.

6.5 Setting Up Your First Scraping Project

To effectively utilize a web scraping framework, it is essential to understand the setup process. Here are the fundamental steps to get started with a scraping project:

Select Your Framework: Choose a scraping framework that aligns with your needs. For instance, ifyou primarily deal with static HTML, Beautiful Soup may suffice. Alternatively, select Scrapy for larger- scale projects.

Install Dependencies: Ensure that the framework and any required libraries are properly installed. This often involves using package managers such as pip for Python or npm for Node.js.

Define Your Target: Identify the websites and specific data points you wish to scrape. Understanding the structure of the target website is crucial in crafting an effective scraping strategy.

Develop the Scraper: Write the code to navigate the website and extract the desired data. Make use of the framework's features to handle errors, store data, and manage requests.

Test and Iterate: Scraping configurations may require adjustments. Test your scraper against thetarget website and refine it based on the results.

Ethics and Compliance: Always consider the ethical implications of your scraping project, ensuringcompliance with legal guidelines and the website's terms of service.

A web scraping framework serves as a vital tool for harnessing the vast potential of online information. By standardizing the scraping process, these frameworks enable developers to address the complexities of data extraction while promoting efficient and responsible practices. In the following chapters, we will delve deeper into implementing specific frameworks, exploring their functionalities, and providing practical examples of web scraping projects.

Setting Up and Configuring Scrapy in Python

Whether you are a data scientist, a web developer, or someone interested in web scraping for research purposes, Scrapy provides the tools required to efficiently scrape web content. This chapter will guide you through the process of setting up and configuring Scrapy for your projects.

1. Prerequisites

Before you begin, ensure that you have the following installed on your system:

Python: Scrapy supports Python 3.6 and above. You can download the latest version from [python.org](https://www.python.org/downloads/).
pip: This is a package manager for Python, which is usually included with Python installations. You can check if you have it by running `pip --version` in your terminal or command prompt.

Check python and pip installations by running:

```bash
python --versionpip --version
```

If you see the respective versions, you are good to go! ## 2. Installing Scrapy
Once you have confirmed that Python and pip are installed, you can install Scrapy. Open your terminal (or command prompt) and run the following command:

```bash
pip install Scrapy
```

This command will download and install the latest version of Scrapy along with its dependencies. ### Verifying the Installation
To ensure that Scrapy has been installed successfully, run the following command:

```bash
scrapy --version
```

You should see something like this:

```
Scrapy 2.xx.x - no active project
```

This output indicates that Scrapy is ready to be used! ## 3. Setting Up a Scrapy Project

Now that Scrapy is installed, you can create your first Scrapy project. Follow these steps: ### Step 1: Create a Project Directory
Choose a location on your file system where you want to place your Scrapy project. Then, navigate to that directory using the terminal and create a new project with the following command:

```bash
scrapy startproject project_name
```

Replace `project_name` with your desired project name. This command will create a new directory with the structure of a Scrapy project, including essential subdirectories and files:

```
project_name/
scrapy.cfg project_name/
__init.py items.py middlewares.pypipelines.py settings.py
```

97

spiders/
```

### Step 2: Understanding the Project Structure

**scrapy.cfg**: This is the project configuration file, which allows you to run Scrapy commands from the project root.
**project_name/**: This is where your Scrapy project's code goes.
**items.py**: This file is where you define the data structure for the items you will scrape.
**middlewares.py**: This file allows you to customize the request/response processing.
**pipelines.py**: This is where you process the scraped data (e.g., saving it to a database or a file).
**settings.py**: This file is for configuring various aspects of Scrapy, including user agents, download delays, and more.
**spiders/**: This directory is where you will create your spider files, which contain the logic for scraping the specific websites.

## 4. Configuring Scrapy Settings

Configurations in Scrapy are primarily done in the `settings.py` file found in your project directory. Here are some common settings you may want to adjust:

### User-Agent

The User-Agent string identifies your Scrapy spider to web servers. You can set it in `settings.py`:
```

```python
USER_AGENT = 'myproject (http://www.example.com)'
```

Download Delay

To avoid overwhelming the website you're scraping, you can set a download delay:

```python
DOWNLOAD_DELAY = 2 # Delay in seconds
```

Concurrent Requests

You may also want to adjust the number of concurrent requests Scrapy makes:

```python
CONCURRENT_REQUESTS = 16 # Default is 16
```

Item Pipelines

If you plan to process items, don't forget to enable pipelines in the settings:

```python ITEM_PIPELINES = {
'project_name.pipelines.YourPipeline': 300,
}
```

5. Creating Spiders

Spiders are the heart of your Scrapy project. They define how Scrapy will scrape the data from the specifiedwebsite.

To create a spider, navigate to the `spiders/` directory and create a new Python file, e.g., `example_spider.py`. Here's a simple example of a spider:

```python
import scrapy

class ExampleSpider(scrapy.Spider):
name = 'example'
start_urls = ['http://quotes.toscrape.com/']

def parse(self, response):
for quote in response.css('div.quote'):yield {
'text': quote.css('span.text::text').get(),
'author': quote.css('span small.author::text').get(),


```
}

next_page = response.css('li.next a::attr(href)').get() if next_page is not None:
yield response.follow(next_page, self.parse)

Running the Spider

To run your spider, navigate back to your project's root directory and execute:

```bash
scrapy crawl example
```

You should see Scrapy start crawling and extracting quotes as defined in the `parse` method.

This chapter has covered the basics of setting up and configuring Scrapy in your Python environment. You learned how to install Scrapy, create a project, understand its structure, make necessary configurations, and create a simple spider. Scrapy is a powerful tool for web scraping, and mastering its intricacies will enable you to extract data from various websites effectively.

Creating Your First Link Scraping Project in Scrapy in Python

Web scraping is an essential skill for data professionals. It allows you to extract information from websites, providing the potential to analyze data or extract valuable insights. In this chapter, we will walk through creating your first web scraping project using Scrapy, a powerful and flexible framework for extracting data from websites in Python. By the end of this chapter, you will have a functional Scrapy project that can scrape links from a website and store them for further analysis.

Prerequisites

Before we start, ensure you have the following prerequisites installed:

Python 3.x
Pip (Python package installer)
Scrapy library

To install Scrapy, you can use pip in your terminal:

```bash
pip install scrapy
```

Once everything is installed, we can begin our project.## Step 1: Setting Up Your Scrapy Project
To create a new Scrapy project, open your terminal and run the following command:

```bash
scrapy startproject link_scraper
```

This command will create a new directory titled `link_scraper`, which contains the following structure:

``` link_scraper/
scrapy.cfg link_scraper/
__init_.py items.py middlewares.pypipelines.py settings.py
spiders/
__init_.py
```

Understanding the Project Structure

scrapy.cfg: This is the configuration file for your Scrapy project.

link_scraper/: This directory contains the actual code for your project.

items.py: This file is where you define the data structure you want to scrape.

middlewares.py: This file contains middleware components that process requests/responses.

pipelines.py: This file is where you define the data processing pipelines.

settings.py: This file allows you to configure the settings for your Scrapy project.

spiders/: This directory will hold your spider scripts.

Step 2: Creating Your First Spider

In Scrapy, a spider is a class that you define to scrape information from a website. Let's create our first spider to extract all the links from the specified webpage.

Navigate to the `spiders` directory:

```bash
cd link_scraper/link_scraper/spiders
```

Now, create a new Python file named `link_spider.py`:

```bash
touch link_spider.py
```

Open `link_spider.py` in your code editor and define the spider as follows:

```python
import scrapy

class LinkSpider(scrapy.Spider):
    name = 'link_spider'
    start_urls = ['http://example.com']  # Replace with the URL you want to scrape

    def parse(self, response):
        # Extract all links from the page
        links = response.css('a::attr(href)').getall()

        # Yield the links as a dictionary
        for link in links:
            yield {'link': link}
```

# Follow pagination links (optional)
next_page = response.css('a.next::attr(href)').get() if next_page is not None:
yield response.follow(next_page, self.parse)

Code Breakdown

name: This is a unique name for your spider. You will use this name to run the spider from the command line.
start_urls: This is a list of URLs where your spider will begin scraping.
parse: This method is called to handle the response of the URL(s) specified in `start_urls`. In this

method, we use CSS selectors to extract all hyperlinks (`<a>` tags) and yield them as items.## Step 3: Running

Your Spider
Now that we have created the spider, we can run it using the command line. Go back to the root directory of your project:

```bash
cd ../../
```

Run the spider with the following command:

```bash
scrapy crawl link_spider -o links.json
```

This command will execute your spider and output the scraped links to a file named `links.json`. The `-o` parameter specifies the output format (which can be JSON, CSV, or XML).

Observing the Output

Once the spider finishes running, open the `links.json` file to see the scraped links in JSON format. This file will contain all the hyperlinks extracted from the specified webpage.

Step 4: Handling Link Quality

In web scraping, it's important to ensure that the links you're collecting are valid and useful. You can filter out junk links like `#`, `javascript:void(0);`, or links that lead to resources you're not interested in. Modify the `parse` method to include a simple filtering mechanism:

```python
def parse(self, response):
links = response.css('a::attr(href)').getall()for link in links:
if link.startswith('http') and link not in ['#', '']:yield {'link':
link}
```

This simple condition will help ensure that only valid, external HTTP links are yielded.

Congratulations! You have successfully created your first web scraping project using Scrapy in Python. In this chapter, you learned how to set up a Scrapy project, create a spider to extract links from a website, run your spider, and filter out unwanted links.

Chapter 7: Advanced Techniques in Scrapy for Efficient Link Scraping

As web data grows increasingly complex and dynamic, mastering advanced techniques in Scrapy can significantly enhance your scraping efficiency, especially when it comes to extracting links from web pages.In this chapter, we will explore several advanced techniques you can implement in Scrapy to optimize your link scraping process.

1. Custom Middlewares for Link Management ### 1.1 The Role of Middlewares

Middlewares in Scrapy act as a bridge between the engine and the spiders, allowing you to perform custom processing of requests and responses. For link scraping, you can create middleware that helps filter, categorize, or manage the links you emit.

1.2 Creating Custom Middlewares

To create a custom middleware, define a class and add it to the `DOWNLOADER_MIDDLEWARES` setting in your `settings.py` file. Here's an example of a middleware that filters out links based on certaincriteria:

```python
class LinkFilterMiddleware:
def process_response(self, request, response, spider):
# This is where you would implement your filtering logic.
# Example: Only allow links from specific domains
allowed_domains = ['example.com', 'anotherexample.com']        for        link        in
```

```
response.css('a::attr(href)').getall():
if any(domain in link for domain in allowed_domains):
yield response.follow(link, self.parse)
return response
```

1.3 Managing Duplicate Links

To avoid processing the same link multiple times, you can leverage Scrapy's built-in
`DUPEFILTER_HTTP` to implement a simple duplicate filter. This can help you maintain a clean dataset by checking for previously visited links before making a new request.

2. Advanced Selector Techniques ### 2.1 CSS and XPath Selectors
Scrapy's powerful selectors allow you to extract links with great precision. Learn to utilize both CSS and XPath selectors effectively. Here's how to extract links more efficiently:

CSS Selectors: Scrapy uses Beautiful Soup for CSS selections. You can chain selectors to refine your target:

```python
links = response.css('div.container a::attr(href)').getall()
```

XPath Selectors: If you are working with more complex structures, XPath provides a robust way to navigate XML documents:

```python
links                                    =
response.xpath('//div[@class="container"]/a/@href').get
all()
```

2.2 Regex for URL Filtering

Sometimes, you may need to extract links that match
specific patterns (e.g., URLs containing a particular query
parameter). Regular expressions (regex) can help here.
Use the `re` module to filter URLs based on patterns:

```python
import re

def filter_links(links):
    pattern                                    =
re.compile(r'https://www\.example\.com/products/\d+')
    return [link for link in links if pattern.match(link)]
```

3. Asynchronous Requests for Faster Crawling

3.1 Understanding Scrapy's Asynchronous Nature

Scrapy is built on Twisted, an asynchronous networking
library. By default, Scrapy handles requests
asynchronously, allowing you to scrape multiple pages
concurrently. This is especially useful when you are
scraping large volumes of links.

3.2 Configuring Concurrency

109

You can control the concurrency of your requests in the `settings.py` file:

```python
# Increase the number of concurrent requests (default is 16)
CONCURRENT_REQUESTS = 32

# Add a delay (in seconds) between requests to avoid overwhelming the server DOWNLOAD_DELAY = 0.5 # Adjust according to the server's tolerance
```

4. Utilizing Scrapy Pipelines for Link Storage

After extracting links efficiently, the next step is to store them. Scrapy pipelines will allow you to streamline this process.

4.1 Creating a Pipeline for Storing Links

Define a custom pipeline to process the links you scraped. You can store the links in a database, CSV file, or any other storage mechanism:

```python
class LinkStoragePipeline:

def process_item(self, item, spider):
# Example: append the link to a CSV file with open('links.csv', 'a') as f:
f.write(f"{item['link']}\n")return item
```

```
```

4.2 Activating the Pipeline

Activate your custom pipeline in the `settings.py` file:

```python
ITEM_PIPELINES = {
'myproject.pipelines.LinkStoragePipeline': 300,
}
```

5. Scrapy Signals for Real-Time Monitoring
5.1 Understanding Scrapy Signals
Scrapy provides signals that allow you to connect to various events in the scraping cycle. By utilizing signals, you can monitor the progress of your spider and react to specific events, such as requests being sent or responses being received.

5.2 Implementing a Signal Handler

You can implement a signal handler to log link extraction or errors in real time:

```python
from scrapy import signals

class LinkScrapingMonitor:
@classmethod
def from_crawler(cls, crawler):obj = cls()
crawler.signals.connect(obj.spider_opened,
signal=signals.spider_opened)
crawler.signals.connect(obj.spider_closed,
```

```
signal=signals.spider_closed) return obj
```

def spider_opened(self, spider): print(f"Spider opened: {spider.name}")

def spider_closed(self, spider): print(f"Spider closed: {spider.name}")
```
```

Custom middlewares, powerful selector strategies, efficient concurrency, robust pipelines, and real-time monitoring all contribute to a more streamlined and effective scraping process. As web scraping continues to evolve, these practices will help you stay ahead, ensuring that your link extraction workflows are both efficient and effective. As you move forward, consider experimenting with these techniques to see how they can be tailored to your specific needs. Happy scraping!

Scraping Multiple Web Pages and Handling Pagination

When dealing with websites that present information across multiple pages, the challenge intensifies as we must not only extract data from a single page but also navigate through multiple pages of content. This chapter will cover the techniques and best practices for scraping multiple web pages and handling pagination using Python, focusing on popular libraries such as `requests` and `BeautifulSoup`.

Understanding Pagination

Before we dive into the code, it's essential to understand what pagination is. Pagination is the process of dividing content into discrete pages. Websites often use pagination to make it easier for users to navigate through large sets of data. A typical example is an e-commerce site displaying products in multiple pages or a blog that shows articles split across several pages.

To effectively scrape a website, we need to identify how the website implements its pagination. There are commonly two approaches:

URL-based Pagination: This method involves changing the URL of the page to load the next set of results. For example, you might see URLs like `example.com/products?page=1`, `example.com/products?page=2`, etc.

AJAX-based Pagination: In this case, the content is loaded dynamically via JavaScript. The user scrolls down or clicks a button, and the browser fetches new data without changing the URL. Scraping AJAX-based content can be more complex and might require using tools like Selenium or Scrapy with proper requests.

Setting Up Your Environment

To start, you will need to have Python installed along with the `requests` and `BeautifulSoup` libraries. If you haven't already installed these, you can do so using pip:

```bash
```

```
pip install requests beautifulsoup4
```

Scraping a Website with URL-based Pagination

Let's go through an example of scraping a website that uses URL-based pagination. For the sake of this example, let's assume we are scraping product data from a fictional e-commerce site. The example URL is `http://example.com/products?page=1`, and it has multiple pages of products.### The Code
Let's write a script that scrapes data from this website.

```python
import requests
from bs4 import BeautifulSoup

# Function to scrape data from a single page
def scrape_page(page_number):

    url = f'http://example.com/products?page={page_number}'
    response = requests.get(url)

    # Check if the page is accessible
    if response.status_code != 200:
        print(f"Failed to retrieve page {page_number}")
        return None

    soup = BeautifulSoup(response.text, 'html.parser')

    # Assuming each product is contained in a div with class 'product'
    products = soup.find_all('div', class_='product')
```

```python
    product_list = []
    for product in products:
        title = product.find('h2').text
        price      =      product.find('span',      class_='price').text
        product_list.append({
        'title': title, 'price': price
        })

    return product_list

# Function to scrape multiple pages
def scrape_multiple_pages(start_page, end_page):
    all_products = []
    for   page   in   range(start_page,   end_page   +   1):
    print(f'Scraping page {page}...')
    products = scrape_page(page) if products:
    all_products.extend(products)return all_products
# Scrape product data from pages 1 to 5
all_products = scrape_multiple_pages(1, 5)

# Output the scraped data for product in all_products:
print(f"Product:          {product['title']},          Price:
{product['price']}")
```

Explanation of the Code

Imports: We import the necessary libraries for making HTTP requests and parsing HTML.

scrape_page Function: This function takes a `page_number` as an argument, constructs the URL, and requests the page's content. If the response is successful, it

115

parses the HTML to extract product details such as title and price.

scrape_multiple_pages Function: This function loops through a given range of pages, calling `scrape_page` for each page. It collects all products into a single list.

Execution: We call the `scrape_multiple_pages` function for pages 1 through 5 and print the product details.

Handling Potential Issues ### Rate Limiting
When scraping multiple pages, it's essential to be respectful to the website's resources. Websites often implement rate limiting to prevent abuse. Consider adding a delay (using `time.sleep()`) between requests:

```python import time

time.sleep(2) # Delay for 2 seconds between requests
```

Error Handling

It's important to implement error handling for various scenarios, such as network issues or changes in the webpage structure. Always check the status code and handle exceptions appropriately.

Web Scraping Ethics

Before scraping a website, always review its `robots.txt`

file to ensure you are allowed to scrape the site. Respect any guidelines set by the website, and refrain from causing undue load on its servers.

We explored techniques to construct URLs for different pages and developed a simple Python script to extract data from an e-commerce product page. As you continue your web scraping journey, remember to follow best practices regarding ethics, legality, and performance optimization. In the next chapter, we will dive into more advanced web scraping topics, including handling AJAX requests and utilizing scraping frameworks.

Handling JavaScript and AJAX-Driven Web Pages

Unlike traditional static web pages, which require a full refresh to load new content, AJAX empowers developers to send and retrieve data asynchronously without disrupting the user experience. This chapter delves into the intricacies of handling JavaScript and AJAX-driven web pages, discussing methodologies for ensuring seamless interactions, effective debugging, and maintaining accessibility.

Understanding JavaScript and AJAX ### JavaScript Basics
JavaScript is a versatile programming language that runs on the client side, allowing developers to create dynamic content and interactive features. Key features of JavaScript include:

Event Handling: JavaScript can respond to user actions such as clicks, keystrokes, and mouse movements, enabling developers to create engaging experiences.

DOM Manipulation: The Document Object Model (DOM) represents the structure of a web page, allowing developers to interact with and modify HTML elements dynamically.

AJAX Integration: JavaScript can be used in conjunction with AJAX to communicate with the server and update parts of a web page without requiring a full reload.

AJAX Fundamentals

AJAX is a set of web development techniques that enable asynchronous data transmission between the client and server. Key components of AJAX include:

XMLHttpRequest Object: The core of AJAX, this JavaScript object enables the sending of HTTP requests to the server in the background.

JSON (JavaScript Object Notation): While originally AJAX used XML for data transfer, JSON has become the de facto standard due to its lightweight nature and easy integration with JavaScript.

Key Concepts in Handling AJAX Requests ### Making an AJAX Request

Making an AJAX request involves the following steps:

Create an XMLHttpRequest Object:

```javascript
var xhr = new XMLHttpRequest();
```

Configure the Request:

```javascript
xhr.open('GET', 'https://api.example.com/data', true);
```

Define a Callback Function:

```javascript
xhr.onload = function() { if (xhr.status === 200) {
var      data      =      JSON.parse(xhr.responseText);
console.log(data);
}
};
```

Send the Request:

```javascript
xhr.send();
```

Handling Responses

Handling responses involves checking the status of the request and processing the returned data. The `onload` and `onerror` events are crucial for managing successful responses and errors, respectively:

```javascript
```

```javascript
xhr.onerror = function() {
console.error('An error occurred while handling the AJAX request.');
};
```

Updating the DOM Dynamically

Upon receiving data from the server, it's common to update the web page without a full reload. This can be achieved by manipulating the DOM:

```javascript
document.getElementById('content').innerHTML = data.message;
```

Best Practices for JavaScript and AJAX ### 1. Optimize Performance
Minimize Requests: Combine multiple requests where possible to reduce server load. Use techniques like lazy loading for images and additional resources.
Asynchronous Loading: Utilize async and defer attributes for script elements to prevent blocking rendering.

2. Error Handling

Implement robust error handling to enhance user experience. Ensure users receive notifications when errors occur, providing them with the option to retry the action.

3. Accessibility Considerations

AJAX applications must be accessible to all users, including those using assistive technologies:

Use ARIA (Accessible Rich Internet Applications) roles and properties to convey dynamic changes.
Ensure that all interactive elements are keyboard-accessible.

4. Testing and Debugging

Utilize browser developer tools to debug JavaScript and AJAX interactions. Look for commonly occurring issues such as missing resources, JavaScript errors, and issues with AJAX requests.

```javascript
console.log('AJAX Request sent');xhr.send();
```

5. Frameworks and Libraries

Consider using libraries and frameworks like jQuery, Axios, or Fetch API, which can simplify AJAX calls and handle cross-browser compatibility issues effectively.

Common Scenarios and Solutions

Scenario 1: Content Loading on Demand

Imagine a scenario where users may want to load additional content without refreshing the page—typical in infinite scrolling or pagination. Here's how to handle it:

```javascript
window.onscroll = function() {
if (window.innerHeight + window.scrollY >=
document.body.offsetHeight) {loadMoreContent();
}
};

function loadMoreContent() {
var xhr = new XMLHttpRequest();
xhr.open('GET', 'https://api.example.com/more-data',
true);xhr.onload = function() {
if (xhr.status === 200) {
var newContent = JSON.parse(xhr.responseText);
document.getElementById('content').innerHTML +=
newContent.html;
}
};
xhr.send();
}
```

Scenario 2: Form Submission without Page ReloadTo submit a form using AJAX:
```javascript
document.getElementById('myForm').onsubmit =
function(event) {event.preventDefault(); // Prevent the
default form submission var xhr = new
XMLHttpRequest();
xhr.open('POST', 'https://api.example.com/submit',
true); xhr.setRequestHeader('Content-Type',
'application/json');

xhr.onload = function() {
```

```
if (xhr.status === 200) {
alert('Form submitted successfully!');
}
};

var formData = JSON.stringify({
name:  document.getElementById('name').value, email:
document.getElementById('email').value
});

xhr.send(formData);
};
` ` `
```

Handling JavaScript and AJAX-driven web pages is essential for any modern web developer seeking to create fluid, interactive applications. By understanding the mechanics of AJAX, implementing best practices,focusing on accessibility, and utilizing debugging tools, developers can build responsive web pages that cater to user needs while maintaining optimal performance. As the web continues to evolve, mastering these techniques will remain a valuable asset in the developer's toolkit.

Chapter 8: Using Selenium for Dynamic Web LinkScraping

As such, traditional web scraping techniques, which work primarily by fetching static HTML content, can often fall short when dealing with dynamic content. This chapter delves into how to effectively use Selenium, a powerful library that can automate web browsers, to scrape links and data from such dynamicsites.

8.1 Introduction to Selenium

Selenium is a widely used open-source tool for automating web applications for testing purposes. However, its capabilities extend beyond testing; it can be incredibly useful for web scraping, especially for pages that load content dynamically. Unlike other libraries such as Beautiful Soup or Requests, which are excellent forstatic content, Selenium can interact with JavaScript-heavy websites, simulating real user actions like clicking buttons and navigating pages.

8.1.1 Setting Up Selenium

Before diving into the code, let's ensure that you have the necessary tools installed.

Install Selenium: You can install Selenium via pip. Use the following command in your terminal orcommand prompt:
```bash
pip install selenium
```

```
```

Web Driver: Selenium requires a web driver to interface with the selected browser. Chrome and Firefox are two popular choices, and you'll need to download the respective driver and ensure that it is included in your PATH.

For Chrome, download the ChromeDriver that matches your Chrome version from [here](https://sites.google.com/chromium.org/driver/). For Firefox, download GeckoDriver from [here](https://github.com/mozilla/geckodriver/releases).
8.2 Starting with Selenium
Once you have everything installed, let's set up a basic Selenium script to visit a webpage.

```python
from selenium import webdriver

# Set up the Chrome driver driver = webdriver.Chrome()

# Navigate to a webpage driver.get('https://example.com')

# Do something with the page's content print(driver.title)
```

```
# Close the browserdriver.quit()
```

This simple script opens a Chrome browser instance, navigates to 'https://example.com', prints the page title, and then closes the browser.

8.3 Scraping Dynamic Content

Let's consider a real-world scenario where we want to scrape links from a webpage that dynamically loads its content via JavaScript.

8.3.1 Example: Scraping Links from a Dynamic Page

Imagine a webpage that loads a list of articles where links appear only after scrolling. We'll write a script to collect these links.

```python
from selenium import webdriver
from selenium.webdriver.common.by import By from
selenium.webdriver.common.keys import Keys import
time

# Set up the Chrome driver driver = webdriver.Chrome()

# Navigate to a dynamic webpage
driver.get("https://example.com/articles")

# Give it some time to load contenttime.sleep(5)

# Scroll down to load all articles
```

```
body = driver.find_element(By.TAG_NAME, 'body')for _
in range(10): # scroll down 10 times
body.send_keys(Keys.PAGE_DOWN)time.sleep(1)

# Extract article links
article_links = driver.find_elements(By.TAG_NAME, 'a')

for link in article_links:
print(link.get_attribute('href'))

# Close the browserdriver.quit()
```

8.3.2 Explanation of the Code

Navigation: Similar to our earlier script, we navigate
to the target webpage.
Dynamic Loading: By simulating scroll actions with
`Keys.PAGE_DOWN`, we prompt the webpage to load
additional content dynamically.
Extracting Links: Using `find_elements`, we gather
all anchor elements on the page and print their

URLs.

8.4 Handling Waits

One common challenge in scraping dynamic content is timing. Elements may not be immediately available, leading to errors. Selenium provides both implicit and explicit waits to handle this issue.

8.4.1 Implicit Waits

Implicit waits tell Selenium to poll the DOM for a certain amount of time when trying to find an element if it's not immediately available.

```python
driver.implicitly_wait(10) # seconds
```

8.4.2 Explicit Waits

Explicit waits are more flexible and allow you to wait for specific conditions to occur before proceeding.

```python
from selenium.webdriver.support.ui import WebDriverWait
from selenium.webdriver.support import expected_conditions as EC

# Wait until an element is present
element = WebDriverWait(driver, 10).until(
EC.presence_of_element_located((By.ID,
```

```
'dynamicElementId'))
)
```

Selenium opens up a robust avenue for scraping dynamic web pages that would otherwise be inaccessible to simpler scraping libraries. With the ability to interact with web elements, handle AJAX content, and simulate user behavior, it provides a versatile toolkit for data extraction.

Automating Web Browsers with Selenium

Businesses and developers are recognizing the importance of automating repetitive tasks such as web scraping, testing web applications, and generating reports. One of the most popular tools for web automation is Selenium. This chapter introduces Selenium, explaining its core functionalities, setting it up, and exploring practical examples to enhance your web automation capabilities.

What is Selenium?

Selenium is an open-source automation framework used for testing web applications across different browsers and platforms. It provides a suite of tools and libraries that allow developers to write scripts in various programming languages, including Python, Java, C#, Ruby, and JavaScript. The primary components of the Selenium suite include:

Selenium WebDriver: This component allows for the automation of web applications by communicating directly with the browser. It translates commands from the test scripts into browser actions.

Selenium IDE: A record-and-playback tool for creating quick tests without the need for programming. It provides a user-friendly interface that allows users to record their interactions with the browser.

Selenium Grid: A tool for running tests on multiple browsers and devices simultaneously, enabling parallel test execution and speeding up the testing process.

Setting Up Selenium

Before diving into the coding aspect, we need to set up our environment. Below are the steps to install Selenium and get started with a simple automation project.

Step 1: Installing Selenium

To install Selenium, use the package manager Python's `pip`. Open your terminal or command prompt and run:

```bash
pip install selenium
```

Step 2: Setting Up Browser Drivers

Selenium requires a driver to interface with the chosen browser. You'll need to download the driver that corresponds to the browser you wish to use:

Chrome: Download ChromeDriver from the [official site](https://sites.google.com/a/chromium.org/chromedriver/downloads).
Firefox: Download GeckoDriver from the [GitHub releases page](https://github.com/mozilla/geckodriver/releases).
Edge: Download Edge WebDriver from the [official site](https://developer.microsoft.com/en- us/microsoft-edge/tools/webdriver/).

Ensure the driver executable is in your system's PATH for easy access. ### Step 3: Writing Your First Selenium Script

With the setup complete, let's write a simple Python script that automates a web browser to navigate to a webpage. Create a new Python file named `automate.py` and add the following code:

```python
from selenium import webdriver
from selenium.webdriver.common.by import By

# Create a new instance of the Chrome driver driver =
webdriver.Chrome()

#        Navigate        to        a        webpage
driver.get("https://www.example.com")

# Find an element (an example of finding an element by
its tag) heading = driver.find_element(By.TAG_NAME,
"h1") print("Page Heading:", heading.text)
```

```
# Close the browserdriver.quit()
```

This script does the following:

Initializes a new Chrome browser instance.
Navigates to "https://www.example.com".
Locates the first `<h1>` tag on the page and prints its text.
Closes the browser.

Step 4: Understanding WebDriver Commands

Selenium WebDriver provides several commands to interact with web elements. Here are some important functions and their usage:

`.get(url)`: Loads a web page.
`.find_element(by, value)`: Locates a single web element based on specified criteria.
`.find_elements(by, value)`: Locates multiple web elements and returns a list.
`.click()`: Simulates a mouse click on the element.
`.send_keys(keys)`: Sends keys to an input field, simulating keyboard input.
`.text`: Returns the visible text of an element.
`.quit()`: Closes the browser and ends the WebDriver session.## Advanced Web Automation
While the basic example illustrates important principles, real-world scenarios demand more complexautomation solutions. Below are some advanced techniques you may encounter:

1. Handling Dynamic Elements

Web applications often include dynamic content that may not be immediately available. Utilize Selenium's explicit waits to handle such elements efficiently:

```python
from selenium.webdriver.common.by import By
from selenium.webdriver.support.ui import WebDriverWait
```

```python
from selenium.webdriver.support import
expected_conditions as EC

# Wait for an element to be present on the pageelement =
WebDriverWait(driver, 10).until(
EC.presence_of_element_located((By.ID,
"dynamicElementId"))
)
```

2. Navigating Through Pages

Many applications have pagination. Automate navigation through multiple pages by finding and clicking the "Next" button:

```python
while True:
# Perform operations on the current page# ...

try:
next_button = driver.find_element(By.LINK_TEXT,
"Next")next_button.click()
except:
break # Exit loop if "Next" button is not found
```

3. Taking Screenshots

Selenium allows you to capture screenshots of your automated tasks:

```python
driver.save_screenshot("screenshot.png")
```

This can be especially useful for debugging.

Selenium provides powerful capabilities for automating web browsers, helping to increase efficiency and accuracy in web application testing and data collection. As you explore the breadth of Selenium's functionalities, you'll find yourself capable of automating intricate web interactions that save time and reduce errors.

Extracting Links from Dynamic and Interactive Websites with Python

These frameworks enhance user experience by loading content asynchronously and modifying the DOM as users interact with the page. While this interactivity is beneficial for end users, it complicates the tasks of data extraction, particularly link extraction. In this chapter, we will explore techniques for effectively extracting links from these dynamic websites using Python.

Understanding the Challenges

Traditional web scraping methods, which primarily rely on static HTML parsing (using libraries like BeautifulSoup), are often insufficient for dynamic content. When you request a page with a typical HTTP client like `requests`, you may only receive the initial HTML; any content loaded after the page has rendered is not included in that response. To navigate these challenges, we need to adopt different strategies based on the specific technologies employed by the website.

Tools and Libraries Required

Before we dive into the practical aspects of link extraction from dynamic websites, it's important to set up our environment with the necessary tools. The following libraries should be installed:

Requests: To handle HTTP requests.
BeautifulSoup: For parsing HTML and XML documents.
Selenium: For automating web browsers.
Pandas (optional): For storing the extracted links in a structured format.

Install these packages using pip:

```bash
pip install requests beautifulsoup4 selenium pandas
```

Setting Up Selenium

To utilize Selenium, you will also need a web driver that corresponds to the browser you wish to automate. For example, if using Chrome, you'll need ChromeDriver. Make sure to download it from [ChromeDriver's official site](https://sites.google.com/chromium.org/driver/downloads) and ensure it's accessible in your system's PATH.

Extracting Links Using Selenium ### Step 1: Browser Automation
Executing a few basic commands with Selenium allows us

to automate a web browser and handle dynamiccontent effectively. Let's see how to open a browser and navigate to a specific URL.

```python
from selenium import webdriver
from selenium.webdriver.common.by import By
from selenium.webdriver.chrome.service import Service

from selenium.webdriver.chrome.options import Options
from webdriver_manager.chrome import ChromeDriverManager

# Set options for headless mode (optional) options = Options()
options.headless = True

# Set up the web driver
service = Service(ChromeDriverManager().install())
driver = webdriver.Chrome(service=service, options=options)

# Open the webpage
url = 'https://example.com'driver.get(url)
```

Step 2: Extracting Links

After the page has fully loaded, you can extract the links available on that page. Here's how to implementthis:

```python
# Give the page some time to load
```

```python
driver.implicitly_wait(10)

# Find all anchor tags (<a>) in the rendered HTMLlinks =
driver.find_elements(By.TAG_NAME, 'a')

# Retrieve the href attribute for each link
extracted_links = [link.get_attribute('href') for link in
links if link.get_attribute('href') is not None]
```

Step 3: Storing Links

Once we have the links extracted, we might want to save
them for further analysis. Using Pandas, we can easily
store the links in a DataFrame and export it to CSV.

```python
import pandas as pd

# Create a DataFrame
links_df          =          pd.DataFrame(extracted_links,
columns=['Links'])

# Save to CSV links_df.to_csv('extracted_links.csv',
index=False)

print(f"Extracted {len(extracted_links)} links.")
```

Step 4: Closing the Browser

It is important to ensure that we close the browser
instance to free up resources.

```python
# Close the browser

driver.quit()
```

Handling JavaScript-triggered Events

Some interactive websites load content based on user actions, such as scrolling or clicking buttons. To handle these scenarios, you may simulate user interactions with Selenium.

Example: Clicking a Button

```python
# Example of clicking a button to reveal additional links
button = driver.find_element(By.ID, 'loadMoreButton')
button.click()

# Wait for the new content to load
driver.implicitly_wait(10)

# Extract new links again
new_links = driver.find_elements(By.TAG_NAME, 'a')
```

Alternative Options: API Endpoints

In some cases, websites powered by JavaScript may also expose APIs to fetch content dynamically. During your exploration of the website, use the browser's developer tools to inspect network traffic and identify any API requests. If found, you may directly request data from these endpoints using the `requests` library.

```python
import requests

response = requests.get('https://example.com/api/links')
data = response.json()
```

This chapter covered the fundamental steps required to use Selenium for web scraping, as well as alternative strategies like leveraging API endpoints. As you tackle your next web scraping project, keep in mind that each website may present unique challenges, requiring a tailored approach and a mix of different techniques. Always be mindful of the website's terms of service and ethical scraping practices as you gather data from the web.

Chapter 9: Efficient Data Organization andStorage

However, the value derived from web scraping is largely reliant on the methods employed to organize and store the collected data. In Chapter 9, we will explore the various strategies and best practices for efficient data organization and storage in web scraping projects. We will address the importance of data architecture, delve into different storage options, and outline various approaches to ensure your scraped data is comprehensive, accurate, and easily accessible.

9.1 The Importance of Data Organization

Before diving into storage solutions, it is critical to understand why efficient data organization is paramount. Disorganized data can lead to issues such as redundancy, difficulty in retrieval, and inefficiencies in analytics. A well-structured dataset enables quick access to information, eases data manipulation processes, and enhances the overall quality of insights derived from the data. Key aspects of data organization in web scraping include:

9.1.1 Data Integrity

Data integrity refers to the accuracy and consistency of data over its lifecycle. This is vital when scraping data from various sources, as inconsistencies may arise from differing formats, updates, or even incomplete data. Implementing validation steps during the scraping process ensures that you capture accurate and reliable information, reducing errors in your final dataset.

9.1.2 Schema Design

A well-defined schema acts as a blueprint for your data storage, dictating how different elements relate to each other. Consider carefully how you structure your data by categorizing it into logical segments such as user data, product information, or transaction records. A consistent schema aids in maintaining data reliability and simplifies future data integration and querying processes.

9.1.3 Metadata Management

Metadata provides information about other data, helping to contextualize and bring meaning to your dataset. Maintaining accurate and detailed metadata can greatly enhance data usability—indicating the source of the data, the date of scraping, and the relevant attributes. This is especially important for large datasets that maybe used by various stakeholders over time.

9.2 Choosing the Right Storage Solution

Once data organization is established, the next step is to determine the most suitable storage solution. The choice will depend on several factors, including data volume, frequency of access, and analytical requirements. Below are common storage solutions used in web scraping:

9.2.1 Relational Databases

Relational databases, such as MySQL, PostgreSQL, and SQLite, are ideal for structured data that requires strict adherence to predefined schemas. They support complex queries and relationships between data tables,allowing for efficient data management. Relational databases are an excellent choice for applications where data integrity and transactional support are crucial.

9.2.2 NoSQL Databases

For unstructured or semi-structured data that may evolve over time, NoSQL databases like MongoDB or Couchbase offer more flexibility. They allow for dynamic schema design and are well-suited for handling large volumes of data that require horizontal scaling. NoSQL databases are advantageous in scenarios where quick iterations and adaptability are essential.

9.2.3 Flat Files

In some cases, particularly for small-scale scraping projects, flat file storage such as CSV, JSON, or XML files may suffice. This approach is simple to implement and easy to manage, although it can become cumbersome as the data grows in size and complexity. Flat files often work best for lightweight applicationsor when the overhead of a database is not justified.

9.2.4 Cloud Storage

With the growing emphasis on scalability and accessibility, cloud storage solutions like Amazon S3, GoogleCloud Storage, and Azure Blob Storage have risen in popularity. Cloud storage offers flexibility in handling large data sets, provides robust security options, and enables easy integration with other cloud-based services. It's an excellent choice for projects that require high availability and collaboration across teams.

9.3 Data Retrieval and Processing

Efficient data organization and storage should also consider how data can be retrieved and processed. Implementing indexing strategies can significantly improve access speed, particularly in large datasets. Utilizing tools like Elasticsearch for fast search capabilities can minimize latency when querying vast amounts of scraped data.

9.3.1 Query Optimization

Once data is stored, optimizing how queries retrieve and manipulate data becomes essential. Techniques such as indexing, partitioning, and caching can enhance the performance of your database operations.
Choosing the right query structure and understanding your data access patterns can lead to significant performance improvements.

9.3.2 Data Cleaning and Transformation

Before analyzing the scraped data, it's crucial to clean and transform it into a usable format. This may include removing duplicates, handling missing values, and converting data types. Implementing ETL (Extract, Transform, Load) processes can streamline this, ensuring that your dataset is not only organized but also primed for analysis.

As web scraping continues to evolve with the increasing volume and variety of data available online, the importance of these practices cannot be overstated. A well-organized dataset paves the way for insightful analysis, informed decision-making, and the ability to derive maximum value from the information gathered from the web.

Saving Extracted Links in CSV, JSON, and Databases

Whether you're scraping data from websites, gathering insights from APIs, or collating information from other sources, saving extracted links effectively is crucial. This chapter explores how to store extracted links in three popular data formats: CSV, JSON, and databases using Python. Each method has its own advantages and best use cases, which we will cover in detail.

1. Introduction to Data Storage Formats

Before we dive into the practical examples, let's quickly review the three data storage formats we'll be working with:

CSV (Comma-Separated Values): A plain text format that represents tabular data. It's easy to read and write for both humans and machines, making it a great choice for simple datasets.

JSON (JavaScript Object Notation): A lightweight data interchange format that is easy for humans to read and write and easy for machines to parse and generate. It's most commonly used for web APIs and supports complex nested structures.

Databases: Persistent storage that can handle larger datasets and more complex queries. We'll cover how to use SQLite for small projects, which is lightweight yet powerful.

2. Setting Up the Environment

To follow along, ensure you have Python installed alongside the necessary libraries: `pandas` for CSV handling, `json` for JSON operations, and `sqlite3` for database interactions. You can install pandas using pip if you haven't done so yet.

```bash
pip install pandas
```

Now, let's start with some extracted links, which will serve as our sample data. For the sake of this chapter, let's suppose the following links were extracted from a web scraping script:

```python
extracted_links = [
{"title": "Example Domain", "url": "http://example.com"},
{"title": "Python Official", "url": "https://www.python.org"},
```

```
{"title":        "Stack        Overflow",        "url":
"https://stackoverflow.com"},
]
```

3. Saving Extracted Links in CSV Format

CSV is a great choice for storing tabular data. In this
section, we'll use the `pandas` library to create a
DataFrame from our extracted links and save it as a CSV
file.

Example: Writing to CSV

```python
import pandas as pd

# Sample data extracted_links = [
{"title": "Example Domain", "url": "http://example.com"},
{"title":        "Python        Official",        "url":
"https://www.python.org"},
{"title":        "Stack        Overflow",        "url":
"https://stackoverflow.com"},
]

# Create a DataFrame
df = pd.DataFrame(extracted_links)

#    Save    DataFrame    to    CSV    csv_file_path    =
'extracted_links.csv'                df.to_csv(csv_file_path,
index=False)

print(f'Data saved to {csv_file_path} successfully.")
```

```
```

Output
Running the above code will produce a CSV file named `extracted_links.csv` formatted as follows:

```
title,url
Example Domain,http://example.com
Python Official,https://www.python.org
Stack Overflow,https://stackoverflow.com
```

4. Saving Extracted Links in JSON Format

JSON is ideal for hierarchical data structures. Python's built-in `json` library allows us to easily convert our extracted links into JSON format.

Example: Writing to JSON

```python
import json

# Sample data
extracted_links = [
{"title": "Example Domain", "url": "http://example.com"},
{"title": "Python Official", "url": "https://www.python.org"},
{"title": "Stack Overflow", "url": "https://stackoverflow.com"},
]

# Save data to JSON
json_file_path = 'extracted_links.json'
with open(json_file_path, 'w') as json_file:
```

```
json.dump(extracted_links, json_file, indent=4)

print(f"Data saved to {json_file_path} successfully.")
```

Output
The above code will create a file named `extracted_links.json`, formatted neatly:

```json
[
{
"title": "Example Domain","url": "http://example.com"
},
{
"title": "Python Official",
"url": "https://www.python.org"
},
{
"title": "Stack Overflow",
"url": "https://stackoverflow.com"
}
]
```

5. Saving Extracted Links in a Database

For larger datasets or when more complex queries are required, using a database is advantageous. In this example, we'll use SQLite, a self-contained database engine that requires no setup beyond including the built-in `sqlite3` module.

Example: Storing Data in SQLite

```python
import sqlite3

# Sample data extracted_links = [
{"title": "Example Domain", "url": "http://example.com"},
{"title": "Python Official", "url": "https://www.python.org"},
{"title": "Stack Overflow", "url": "https://stackoverflow.com"},
]

# Connect to SQLite database (it will create one if it
doesn't exist) connection =
sqlite3.connect('extracted_links.db')
cursor = connection.cursor()

# Create a table cursor.execute('''
CREATE TABLE IF NOT EXISTS links ( id INTEGER
PRIMARY KEY,
title TEXT,url TEXT
) ''')

# Insert data into the table for link in extracted_links:
cursor.execute('''

INSERT INTO links (title, url) VALUES (?, ?) ''',
(link['title'], link['url']))

# Commit the changes and close the connection
connection.commit()
connection.close()

print("Data saved to extracted_links.db successfully.")
```

```
```

Verifying the Data

To verify that the data is correctly stored in the database, you can include a query to select all records:

```python
# Reconnect to the database to verify
connection = sqlite3.connect('extracted_links.db')cursor = connection.cursor()

# Fetch and print data cursor.execute('SELECT * FROM links')rows = cursor.fetchall()
for row in rows:
print(row)

connection.close()
```

In this chapter, we covered the essentials of saving extracted links in CSV, JSON, and databases using Python. Each method has its own use case depending on the complexity of your data and your future data access needs.

Organizing and Categorizing Links for Future Use in python

As Python developers, having a systematic way to organize and categorize these links not only enhances productivity but also aids in quick retrieval when needed. In this chapter, we will explore how to effectively organize and categorize links in Python using various data structures and libraries.

Understanding the Importance of Link Organization

Before diving into the implementation, it is essential to understand why organizing links is critical:

Efficiency: Quick retrieval of needed resources saves time.
Focus: Reduces distraction by minimizing the time spent searching for resources.
Resource Management: Keeps your favorite and useful links in one accessible place.
Collaboration: If shared with a team, categorized links promote collaboration and knowledge sharing.## Setting Up the Environment
To follow along with the examples, ensure you have Python installed on your machine. You can use any code editor (like VS Code, PyCharm, or even Jupyter Notebook) of your choice to implement the followingexamples.

Step 1: Choosing Data Structures

The first step in organizing our links is selecting an appropriate data structure. For our purposes, a `dictionary` (for categorization) of lists (to store links) is a suitable choice. This way, we can easily append new links and retrieve them based on their categories.

```python
# Initialize an empty dictionary to hold categories and
```

their respective linkslink_categories = {}
```

### Step 2: Creating Functions to Add and Retrieve Links

Next, we can create functions to add links to categories and retrieve them.

```python
def add_link(category, link):
"""Add a link to a specified category.""" if category in link_categories:
link_categories[category].append(link)else:
link_categories[category] = [link]
print(f"Link added to category '{category}': {link}")

def retrieve_links(category):
"""Retrieve all links for a specified category.""" return link_categories.get(category, [])
```

Step 3: Example Usage

Now that we have our basic functions, let's see them in action.

```python
# Adding links to different categories
add_link("Tutorials", "https://www.learnpython.org")
add_link("Documentation", "https://docs.python.org/3/")      add_link("Tutorials", "https://realpython.com/")              add_link("Tools", "https://pypi.org/")
```
```

```python
# Retrieving links from a specific category
tutorial_links = retrieve_links("Tutorials")
print("Tutorial Links:", tutorial_links)
```

Step 4: Enhancements - Searching and Removing Links

To make our link organizer more robust, we can add more functionalities like searching for links and removing links.

```python
def search_link(keyword):
    """Search for links containing the keyword across all categories."""
    found_links = {}
    for category, links in link_categories.items():
        matches = [link for link in links if keyword in link]
        if matches:
            found_links[category] = matches
    return found_links

def remove_link(category, link):
    """Remove a link from a specified category."""
    if category in link_categories and link in link_categories[category]:
        link_categories[category].remove(link)
        print(f"Link removed from category '{category}': {link}")
    else:
        print(f"The link '{link}' is not found in category '{category}'.")

# Example of searching for links
search_results = search_link("python")
print("Search Results:", search_results)
```

```python
# Example of removing a link
remove_link("Tutorials", "https://www.learnpython.org")
```

Step 5: Persisting Data

While our current implementation works in memory, we will eventually want to save our organized links so they can persist beyond the current session. We can achieve this using Python's built-in `pickle` module to serialize the `link_categories` dictionary.

```python
import pickle

def save_links_to_file(filename):
    """Save the links dictionary to a specified file."""
    with open(filename, 'wb') as file:
        pickle.dump(link_categories, file)
    print(f"Links saved to {filename}")

def load_links_from_file(filename):
    """Load links dictionary from a specified file."""
    global link_categories
    with open(filename, 'rb') as file:
        link_categories = pickle.load(file)
    print(f"Links loaded from {filename}")

# Save the current links to a file
save_links_to_file('links.pkl')

# Load links from the file
load_links_from_file('links.pkl')
```

```
```

In this chapter, we explored how to effectively organize and categorize web links for future use in Python. From setting up a simple dictionary-based system to enhancing it with searching and removal functionalities, we equipped ourselves with practical skills for link management. Additionally, we learned how to ensure the persistence of our data using the `pickle` module.

Chapter 10: Dealing with Web Scraping Challenges

However, as more individuals and organizations deploy scraping techniques, numerous challenges have arisen. This chapter delves into the most common hurdles encountered in web scraping and provides strategies to navigate them effectively.

10.1 Understanding the Legal and Ethical Landscape

Before diving into the technical aspects of web scraping, it is crucial to grasp the legal and ethical considerations. Different jurisdictions have different laws regarding data usage, and websites often have terms of service that explicitly prohibit scraping.

10.1.1 Legal Considerations

Terms of Service: Many websites contain clauses in their terms of service that restrict automated data collection. Scraping a website may breach these terms and lead to legal actions.
Copyright and Data Ownership: Data available on the web can be subject to copyright laws, and unauthorized use may result in litigation.
GDPR and Privacy Laws: Collecting personal data from EU citizens under the General Data Protection Regulation (GDPR) can have severe penalties if not handled properly.

10.1.2 Ethical Scraping

Ethically, web scraping should respect the intentions of site owners and consider the potential impact on their servers. Responsible scrapers avoid overloading the website with frequent requests and instead implement strategies to minimize server strain.

10.2 Overcoming Technical Roadblocks

When it comes to the technical aspects of web scraping, several challenges can significantly impede the process. Below are some of the most common hurdles and suggested solutions.

10.2.1 Anti-Scraping Technologies

Many websites have installed advanced anti-scraping measures to protect their data. These may include:

CAPTCHAs: These tests are designed to determine if a user is human. Bypassing CAPTCHAs can be complicated, but services like 2Captcha or integrating machine learning models can help automate the process.
Rate Limiting: Websites may limit the number of requests an IP address can make over a certain time period. To avoid this, scrapers can:
Utilize multiple IP addresses through proxies.
Implement exponential backoff strategies, reducing the frequency of requests gradually after encountering a limit.

10.2.2 Dynamic Content Loading

With the rise of JavaScript frameworks, many web pages

now load content dynamically. This can hinder traditional scraping methods. Solutions include:

Headless Browsers: Tools like Puppeteer or Selenium can render JavaScript-heavy pages, allowing scrapers to extract dynamically loaded data.
API Access: Investigate whether the site offers an API that provides the required data without the need for scraping.

10.3 Data Quality and Validation

Obtaining data is only one side of the scraping equation; ensuring its quality is equally important. Scrapers may encounter:

10.3.1 Inconsistent Data Formats

Websites may present information in various formats. To handle this:

Data Parsing Libraries: Utilize libraries such as Beautiful Soup or lxml to standardize data extraction.
Regular Expressions: Implement regex patterns for more complex data validation and extraction tasks. ### 10.3.2 Duplicate or Incomplete Data
When scraping multiple pages, it's common to encounter duplicate or incomplete records. Techniques to manage this include:

Hashing: Create hashes for unique records to identify duplicates before data entry.
Data Cleaning: Apply data cleaning methods through

frameworks like Pandas to fill in missing values or eliminate redundancies.

10.4 Keeping Up with Change

Websites are continually evolving, which often alters the structure of their HTML, leading to broken scrapers. To mitigate this issue:

10.4.1 Regular Maintenance

Establish a routine to check and update scraping scripts. Automated monitoring tools can notify you of changes that require attention.

10.4.2 Version Control

Utilize version control systems like Git to maintain your scraping code, allowing for easy tracking and rollback when issues arise.

By being aware of the legal landscape, addressing technical difficulties, ensuring data quality, and maintaining adaptability, practitioners can navigate these challenges effectively. This proactive approach not only increases the success rate of scraping projects but also fosters ethical practices in data collection, ultimately leading to more sustainable and respectful usage of online resources. In the following chapters, we will explore specific web scraping frameworks and best practices for effective deployment.

Handling Rate Limits, CAPTCHAs, and Web Security with Python

As applications increasingly rely on APIs and web scraping, understanding how to manage these challenges with Python becomes essential. This chapter will delve into strategies for handling rate limits, overcoming CAPTCHAs, and reinforcing web security when building applications that interact with web services.

1. Understanding Rate Limits ### 1.1 What are Rate Limits?

Rate limits are restrictions imposed by web services to control the amount of traffic sent or received in a given period. They are implemented to prevent abuse and ensure fair usage among users. Understanding these limits is critical for maintaining access to APIs and web services.

1.2 Common Practices for Handling Rate Limits

Documentation Review: Always refer to the API documentation to understand the specific rate limits for the service you're using.
Throttling Requests: Implement a throttling mechanism in your application to space out requests. This can involve a simple delay using Python's `time.sleep()` function.

```python
import time import requests

def make_request_with_throttle(url): response =
```

```
requests.get(url)
time.sleep(1) # Throttle with a 1-second delay return
response
```

Exponential Backoff: When you encounter a rate-limiting error, use exponential backoff to retry requests. For example, if you receive a 429 status code, wait for a period that doubles with each consecutiveretry.

```python
import time import requests

def make_request_with_backoff(url, retries=5): for i in range(retries):
response = requests.get(url)
if response.status_code == 200:return response
elif response.status_code == 429:
sleep_time = 2 ** i # Exponential backoff
time.sleep(sleep_time)
return None
```

2. Dealing with CAPTCHAs ### 2.1 What are CAPTCHAs?
CAPTCHAs (Completely Automated Public Turing tests to tell Computers and Humans Apart) are challenges designed to prevent bots from accessing web services. They often present distorted letters orimage challenges to distinguish between human users and automated scripts.

2.2 Bypassing CAPTCHAs

While bypassing CAPTCHAs may seem necessary in certain contexts, it is essential to respect the intentions of the web service and seek ethical and legal alternatives.

Manual Solving: Sometimes, manual solving may be required. This can be part of a human-in-the-loop process where you perform other tasks while a human solves the CAPTCHA.
Using CAPTCHA Solving Services: There are third-party services, like 2Captcha, that offer APIs to solve CAPTCHAs programmatically. However, using these services may be against the terms of service of the site, and ethical implications should be carefully considered.

```python
import requests

def solve_captcha(api_key, captcha_image):
response = requests.post('https://2captcha.com/in.php',
data={'key': api_key, 'method': 'post', 'file':
captcha_image})
captcha_id = response.text.split('|')[1] time.sleep(15) #
wait for a while and get the result
response                                    =
requests.get(f'https://2captcha.com/res.php?key={api_ke
y}&action=get&id={captcha_id}')                    return
response.text.split('|')[1] if response.text.startswith('OK|')
else None
```

3. Enhancing Web Security ### 3.1 Securing Your API Keys
When working with APIs, keeping your API keys secure is paramount. Here are best practices:

Environment Variables: Store sensitive information in environment variables using libraries like `python-decouple` or `dotenv`.

```python
from decouple import config

API_KEY = config('API_KEY')
```

Avoid Hardcoding: Never hardcode your API keys in the source code; this exposes them to the publicdomain.

3.2 Rate Limiting Your Services

If you are building an API, you should also implement rate limiting on your end to prevent abuse by users. This can involve tracking requests from users and limiting access based on predetermined thresholds.

3.3 HTTPS and SSL/TLS

Always use HTTPS to encrypt data transmitted between clients and servers. This reduces the risk of data interception and man-in-the-middle attacks, enhancing the security of your application.

3.4 User Authentication and Authorization

Implement standard user authentication methods (e.g., JWT, OAuth) to secure user accounts and sensitiveactions within your applications. This ensures that only authorized users can access certain functionalities.

3.5 Ethical Considerations

Always ensure you are compliant with the laws and terms of service of the web services you interact with. Ethical scraping and API usage involve respecting the service's guidelines and the rights of the data owners.

Handling rate limits, CAPTCHAs, and securing web interactions is an essential aspect of modern web application development. By implementing the strategies discussed, you can build resilient, ethical applications using Python while maintaining the integrity and security of your interactions with web services. Always remember to stay informed about changing regulations and best practices as the landscapeof web security evolves.

Dealing with Blocked Requests and Scraping Detection with Python

As more businesses recognize the value of scraping, they deploy increasingly sophisticated technologies to detect and prevent automated requests. This chapter will delve into the strategies you can employ using Python to avoid getting blocked while scraping websites, as well as tackle detection mechanisms employedby site owners.

5.1 Understanding Scraping Detection

Before you can effectively deal with blocked requests, it's crucial to understand how websites detect scraping behaviors. Common techniques include:

167

Rate Limiting: Websites monitor the frequency of requests coming from an IP address. If too many requests are detected in a short period, the IP may be temporarily or permanently blocked.

User-Agent Analysis: Websites can identify whether requests are coming from real browsers or bots by examining the User-Agent string. Non-standard or default User-Agent strings associated with scraping libraries may raise red flags.

IP Blacklisting: Many websites maintain lists of known IP addresses associated with scraping algorithms. If your IP is on such a list, your requests will be denied.

Behavioral Patterns: Websites can track patterns in navigation, like the speed of scrolling or clicks. Non-human-like behavior can instantly trigger anti-scraping mechanisms.

CAPTCHA Challenges: Some websites employ CAPTCHA to ensure that a user is human before allowing further interaction.

5.2 Strategies for Avoiding Blocks ### 5.2.1 Rotating User-Agents
Switching User-Agent strings for each request can help mimic a regular user. Libraries like `fake_useragent` can generate random User-Agent strings that you can use.

```python
import requests
from fake_useragent import UserAgentua = UserAgent()
```

```python
headers = {
'User-Agent': ua.random
}

response    =    requests.get("https://example.com",
headers=headers)
```

5.2.2 Implementing Rotating Proxies

Using rotating proxies is one of the best ways to avoid IP bans. By routing your requests through different IP addresses, you can distribute your request volume more evenly.

You can use services like Scrapy's `scrapy-rotating-proxies` middleware to manage this:

```python
from scrapy_proxies import ProxyMiddleware

class MySpider(scrapy.Spider):
name = 'example_spider'

def start_requests(self):
urls = ['http://example.com']for url in urls:
yield    scrapy.Request(url=url,    callback=self.parse,
meta={'proxy': 'http://your.proxy.service:port'})

def parse(self, response):# process the responsepass
```

5.2.3 Throttling Requests

To avoid hitting the server too hard and triggering rate limits, implement a delay between requests using the `time.sleep()` function. For example:

```python
import time

for url in url_list:
response = requests.get(url, headers=headers) # process response
time.sleep(2) # sleep for 2 seconds between requests
```

5.2.4 Handling and Bypassing CAPTCHAs

Encounters with CAPTCHAs can stall your scraping efforts. Various services like 2Captcha or Anti-Captcha can be integrated into your scraping script to handle these challenges programmatically.

```python
# Pseudo-code for solving CAPTCHA if 'captcha' in response.text:
captcha_id = solve_captcha(response) # Submit the CAPTCHA solution
```

5.3 Error Handling and Request Retry Logic

When web scraping, it's vital to anticipate errors such as HTTP 403 (Forbidden), 429 (Too Many Requests), or timeouts. Implementing a retry mechanism can enhance your scraper's resilience.

```python
import requests

from requests.exceptions import RequestException
import time

def fetch(url, attempts=5, delay=1):
    for attempt in range(attempts):
        try:
            response = requests.get(url, headers=headers)
            response.raise_for_status()
            return response
        except RequestException as e:
            print(f"Error: {e}. Retrying in {delay} seconds...")
            time.sleep(delay)
    return None

response = fetch("https://example.com")
if response:
    # process response
```

5.4 Ethical Considerations

While the techniques mentioned above can help you avoid detection, it's essential to practice ethical scraping. Always review a website's `robots.txt` file to understand its scraping policies and comply with its terms of service. Responsible scraping minimizes the negative impact on the website and ensures that your efforts are sustainable in the long term.

5.4.1 Respecting Robots.txt

The `robots.txt` file informs crawlers about which pages

they should avoid. Python's `robotparser` can check these rules programmatically.

```python
from urllib.robotparser import RobotFileParser

rp = RobotFileParser()
rp.set_url('http://example.com/robots.txt')rp.read()

if rp.can_fetch('*', 'http://example.com/page'):
response = requests.get('http://example.com/page')
```

Dealing with blocked requests and scraping detection in Python requires a nuanced understanding of web scraping ethics, as well as technical strategies to mimic genuine user behavior while respecting site regulations. By employing techniques like rotating User-Agents, using proxies, throttling requests, and handling errors gracefully, you reduce the risk of getting blocked.

Chapter 11: Error Handling and Debugging in Python Web Scraping

Web scraping has become an indispensable skill for gathering data from the ever-expanding internet. However, scraping isn't just about writing code to extract data; it also involves handling unexpected errors and debugging to ensure the scraper runs smoothly. In this chapter, we will explore error handling and debugging strategies specifically tailored for Python web scraping.

12.1 Understanding Common Errors in Web Scraping

Before delving into strategies for error handling and debugging, it is essential to recognize the common types of errors that may occur during web scraping:

HTTP Errors: Websites may return various HTTP status codes, such as 404 (Not Found), 403 (Forbidden), or 500 (Internal Server Error). Each code indicates a different issue that needs to be addressed.

Connection Errors: These occur when your scraper fails to connect to the target website due to network issues or the site being temporarily down.

Timeouts: When requests take too long to receive a response, a timeout error will occur. It's crucial to set reasonable timeout parameters to avoid indefinite waiting.

Data Parsing Errors: After fetching the page,

attempting to parse the HTML with libraries like BeautifulSoup or lxml might lead to errors if the structure of the HTML is not as expected.

Rate Limiting: Many websites implement rate limiting, which restricts the number of requests from a single IP in a specific timeframe, resulting in a 429 (Too Many Requests) status code.

Element Not Found: If your scraping logic relies on specific HTML elements and they are not present on the page, you'll encounter errors when trying to access them.

12.2 Implementing Error Handling

Effective error handling is critical to building a resilient web scraper. Here are some strategies you can use: ### 12.2.1 Using Try-Except Blocks
In Python, the `try` and `except` blocks are fundamental constructs for managing exceptions. You can wrap your requests and parsing code in `try` blocks to catch specific exceptions and handle them gracefully.

```python
import requests
from bs4 import BeautifulSoup
url = "https://example.com"try:
response = requests.get(url, timeout=5)
response.raise_for_status() # Raises an HTTPError for bad responses soup = BeautifulSoup(response.text, 'html.parser')

# Parsing logic goes here
except requests.exceptions.HTTPError as http_err:
```

```python
    print(f"HTTP error occurred: {http_err}")
except requests.exceptions.ConnectionError as conn_err:
    print(f"Connection error occurred: {conn_err}") except
requests.exceptions.Timeout as timeout_err:
    print(f"Timeout error occurred: {timeout_err}") except
Exception as err:
    print(f"An unexpected error occurred: {err}")
```

12.2.2 Handling Specific Status Codes

When sending a request, you might want to handle
specific HTTP status codes explicitly. For example, you can
create a function to handle retries for 429 status codes.

```python
def fetch_data_with_retries(url, max_retries=3):
retries = 0
while retries < max_retries:try:
response = requests.get(url, timeout=5)
if response.status_code == 429: # Handle Too Many
Requestsprint("Rate limited. Retrying...")
retries += 1
time.sleep(2 ** retries) # Exponential backoffcontinue
response.raise_for_status()return response
except requests.exceptions.RequestException as e:
print(f"Error occurred: {e}")
retries += 1 time.sleep(1)
raise Exception("Max retries exceeded.")
```

12.2.3 Logging Errors

175

Leveraging Python's built-in logging module allows you to maintain a record of errors for later analysis, making it easier to track and debug issues.

```python
import logging
logging.basicConfig(filename='scraper.log',
level=logging.ERROR)try:
response = requests.get(url)
response.raise_for_status()except Exception as e:
logging.error(f"Error occurred while scraping {url}: {e}")
```

12.3 Debugging Techniques

When things go wrong, you need a systematic approach to identify and fix issues. Here are some effective debugging techniques:

12.3.1 Print Statements

Using print statements to track variable values and the flow of your code can help pinpoint where things are failing.

```python
print(f"Fetching data from {url}")
```

12.3.2 Python Debugger (pdb)

You can utilize `pdb`, Python's built-in debugger, to step through your code, inspect variables, and control execution.

```python
import pdb; pdb.set_trace()
```

12.3.3 Use of IDE Debugging Tools

Most modern IDEs, such as PyCharm or VSCode, provide built-in debugging tools that allow breakpoints, variable watches, and more to assist in debugging your code effectively.

12.3.4 Analyzing HTML Responses

If you encounter parsing errors, consider printing the HTML response's content to understand the document's structure better.

```python
print(response.text[:500]) # Print first 500 characters
```

12.4 Best Practices for Reliable Web Scraping

Respect Robots.txt: Always check the website's `robots.txt` file to understand what can and cannot be scraped.

Use User-Agent Headers: Set a user-agent header in your requests to mimic a real web browser, which can help avoid being blocked.

Rate Limiting: Implement delays between requests to

reduce the load on the target server andminimize the risk of being blocked.

Graceful Failures: Ensure your scraper can handle failures gracefully, possibly by storingintermediate results and continuing from the last successful point in case of an error.

Regular Updates: Keep your scraper updated to reflect any changes in the website's HTML structure or APIs.

By employing the strategies discussed in this chapter— such as using try-except blocks, handling specific status codes, logging, and leveraging debugging tools—you can significantly improve the reliability of your scraping projects.

Common Errors in Web Scraping and How to Avoid Them

However, it is not without pitfalls. Understanding common errors in web scraping and devising strategies to avoid them is crucial for successful data extraction. This chapter will outline the typical mistakes that scrapers encounter and provide practical solutions to ensure smooth and effective web scraping processes.
1. Ignoring Website Terms of Service ### Error Overview
Before scraping a website, it's essential to review the website's Terms of Service (ToS). Many sites explicitly prohibit scraping in their policies. Ignoring

these can lead to legal consequences or getting your IP banned.

Avoidance Strategies
Read the ToS: Always take a few moments to read the website's terms. If scraping is prohibited, consider contacting the site owner for permission or explore alternative data sources.
Respect robots.txt: Check the website's `robots.txt` file, which indicates which parts of the site can be crawled or scraped. This file can provide guidance on what is permissible.

2. Not Implementing User-Agent Rotation ### Error Overview
Websites often use User-Agent strings to identify and block automated scripts. If a scraping script uses the same User-Agent on repeated requests, it may get blocked.

Avoidance Strategies
User-Agent Rotation: Utilize libraries that allow for rotating User-Agent strings to mimic different browsers. A library like `fake-useragent` in Python can be helpful.
Random Delay Between Requests: Introduce random time intervals between requests to reduce the chances of being flagged as a bot.

3. Failing to Handle Rate Limits ### Error Overview
Many websites implement rate limits to prevent excessive requests from a single user. Failing to respect these limits can temporarily or permanently ban your IP address.

Avoidance Strategies

Implement Backoff Strategies: Use exponential backoff techniques to gradually increase the time between requests if receiving error codes indicating rate limiting (e.g., HTTP 429).
Monitor Responses: Implement logic to monitor response codes and alter your scraping frequency based on the server's feedback.
4. Hard-Coding Selectors ### Error Overview
Scraping scripts often rely on HTML selectors (like CSS classes and IDs) to access data. If these selectors change, the script breaks.

Avoidance Strategies
Use More Flexibility in Selectors: Instead of hard-coding specific selectors, consider using more generalized XPath queries or CSS selectors that are less likely to change.

Validate Selectors Periodically: Regularly review the structure of the target website to ensure selectors remain valid. Ideally, you should maintain a central repository of your selector mappings.

5. Overlooking Data Structure Changes ### Error Overview
Websites frequently change their layout or content structure, which can lead to broken scrapers. If your
script is dependent on specific structures, it can fail without warning.

Avoidance Strategies
Dynamic Parsing Logic: Develop your scraping logic to be adaptable. Use patterns to identify the data context rather than fixed positions or structures.

Regularly Test Scripts: Schedule regular checks of your scraping script to catch any breaks caused by changes in the website layout.

6. Not Managing Data Ethics and Privacy ### Error Overview
Scraping personal data can raise ethical and legal issues. Failing to consider the implications of data usage,
especially with GDPR and similar regulations, can have serious consequences.

Avoidance Strategies
Anonymize Data: Where possible, anonymize personal data and collect only the information necessary

181

for your application.

Stay Informed of Regulations: Familiarize yourself with laws surrounding data privacy in your jurisdiction and those of the target website's location.

7. Poor Error Handling### Error Overview
Many scrapers do not implement comprehensive error-handling mechanisms. This can lead to unhandled exceptions, causing the entire script to crash or miss data.

Avoidance Strategies
Implement Robust Exception Handling: Use try-except blocks to gracefully handle exceptions and log errors for further analysis without stopping the entire process.

Retries and Fallbacks: Incorporate retry mechanisms for failed requests and consider fallback strategies, such as alternate data sources, to ensure continuity.

8. Neglecting Data Quality### Error Overview
It's tempting to extract data quickly, but overlooking data validation can lead to inconsistencies and garbage data.

Avoidance Strategies
Data Cleaning: Implement data cleaning procedures post-scraping to standardize formats, remove duplicates, and validate data integrity.

Validation Checks: Regularly run validation checks on scraped data to ensure accuracy and quality before populating databases or making decisions based on that data.

Web scraping can be a powerful tool for data extraction, but it must be approached with caution and diligence. By being aware of common errors and the strategies to avoid them, you can mitigate risks associated with scraping. Continue to refine your techniques, stay updated on best practices, and ensure thatyour web scraping endeavors are ethical, legal, and effective. Through careful planning and execution, you can harness the vast resources of the web without encountering the common pitfalls that hound novice scrapers.

Debugging Techniques for Complex Web ScrapingProjects

However, as projects grow in complexity, debugging these scraping scripts can become an arduous task. In this chapter, we will delve into effective debugging techniques specifically tailored for complex web scraping projects, equipping you with the tools and knowledge to tackle common issues and streamline yourworkflow.

Understanding the Basics of Web Scraping

Before diving into debugging techniques, it's essential to understand the foundational elements of web scraping. Web scraping typically involves sending HTTP requests to a server, retrieving HTML content, andthen parsing that content to extract relevant data. While the process seems straightforward, myriad issues may arise due to changes in website structure, missing or inconsistent data, and more.

Common Challenges in Web Scraping

Website Structure Changes: Websites frequently undergo redesigns, which can break your existingscraping logic.
Dynamic Content: Many websites load content dynamically using JavaScript, making it invisible to traditional scraping methods.
Rate Limiting and CAPTCHA: Rapidly scraping a site can lead to IP bans, CAPTCHA challenges, orother forms of blocking.
Data Inconsistencies: Variability in data formats can complicate parsing and data integrity checks.
Connection Issues: Temporary network issues can result in failed requests or incomplete dataretrieval.

Debugging Techniques

Given the potential pitfalls, robust debugging strategies become vital. Here are some effective techniquestailored for complex web scraping projects:

1. Logging

Establish a Logging Framework: Utilize logging libraries such as `logging` in Python to track the execution flow of your scraping script. Log key events such as successful data retrieval, HTTP response codes, and errors encountered.

```python
import logging

# Configure logging
```

```python
logging.basicConfig(level=logging.INFO,
filename='scraper.log', format='%(asctime)s -
%(levelname)s - %(message)s')

logging.info('Starting the scraping process')
```

2. HTTP Status Code Monitoring

Always monitor HTTP response codes. A non-200 response could indicate issues such as forbidden access or resource not found. Use conditional statements to handle unexpected responses gracefully.

```python
response = requests.get(url)
if response.status_code != 200:
logging.error(f"Failed to retrieve {url}, status code: {response.status_code}")else:
# Proceed with data extraction
```

3. Use of Debugging Tools

Utilize debugging tools that allow you to inspect network traffic and evaluate JavaScript execution. Browser developer tools (such as Chrome DevTools) can help identify dynamic content and understand the request/response cycle.

4. Break Down the Scraping Task

For complex projects, break the scraping task into smaller

components. Test each component independently to isolate issues. For example, first ensure your requests are working, then verify HTML parsing, and finally check data validation.

5. Mocking and Stubs

When dealing with temporary issues (like network errors or server downtime), consider using mocking libraries (e.g., `responses` or `unittest.mock` in Python) to simulate responses. This approach allows you to test your parsing logic without needing to perform network requests constantly.

```python
from unittest.mock import patch

@patch('requests.get')
def test_scraping(mock_get):
    mock_get.return_value.status_code = 200
    mock_get.return_value.text = "<html><div class='data'>Sample Data</div></html>"

    # Your scraping logic here
```

6. Detailed Exception Handling

Implement comprehensive exception handling to catch and log unexpected errors. Make use of specific exceptions rather than broad ones to pinpoint precise issues.

```python
try:
```

```python
# Scraping logic here
except requests.exceptions.HTTPError as http_err:
logging.error(f'HTTP error occurred: {http_err}')
except Exception as err: logging.error(f'An error
occurred: {err}')
```

7. Data Validation and Consistency Checks

After data extraction, run validation checks to ensure the
data meets your criteria. This might involve checking for
null values, incorrect data formats, or unexpected data
types.

```python
def validate_data(data):
if not isinstance(data, dict): logging.error('Data is not a
dictionary')
if 'required_field' not in data: logging.error('Missing
required field in data')
```

8. Iterative Development and Testing

Adopt an iterative approach to development. Regularly
test and refine your scripts as you progress. Use version
control systems like Git to track changes, allowing you to
revert to last-known-good configurationsif necessary.

Debugging complex web scraping projects can be a
daunting task, but with a structured approach and the
right techniques, you can navigate the challenges
effectively. By leveraging logging, monitoring HTTP status

codes, utilizing debugging tools, and incorporating detailed error handling, you will be better equipped to maintain robust and effective scraping scripts. As web technologies evolve, keeping your skills and strategies up to date will ensure that your web scraping projects remain successful and sustainable.

Chapter 12: Building a Complete Web Link Scraping Tool

Web scraping is an essential skill for data collection and analysis, and it can help you gather information from various online resources for many purposes, including research, market analysis, and content aggregation.

We will cover the fundamental concepts of web scraping, essential libraries in Python, and the ethical considerations surrounding this practice. By the end of this chapter, you will have a working web link scraper that can efficiently extract all hyperlinks from a given webpage.

Understanding Web Scraping

Web scraping involves extracting information from

websites. While many sites provide APIs for structured data access, not all do. Scraping is particularly useful for getting data from sites that are publicly accessible but lacking structured APIs.

Basic Concepts

HTML and the DOM: Websites are built using HTML (Hypertext Markup Language), which structures content and elements. Understanding the Document Object Model (DOM) is crucial, as it represents the structure of a webpage, making it easier to navigate and select elements.
HTTP Requests: Scraping typically begins with sending HTTP requests to a server to retrieve webpage content. The response is usually an HTML document representing the requested page.
Parsing HTML: After obtaining the HTML document, we need to parse it to extract relevant information, such as links, images, and text.

Required Libraries

For our web link scraping tool, we'll employ several powerful libraries in Python:

Requests: This library simplifies HTTP requests, enabling us to send and receive data from a website effortlessly.
Beautiful Soup: A popular library for parsing HTML and XML documents, Beautiful Soup allows us to navigate the DOM easily.
Pandas: We can use Pandas to structure the extracted data efficiently and save it into desired formats (CSV,

Excel, etc.).

You can install these libraries using pip:

```bash
pip install requests beautifulsoup4 pandas
```

Step-by-Step Implementation

In this section, we will go through building the link scraping tool step by step. ### Step 1: Import Required Libraries

```python
import requests
from bs4 import BeautifulSoupimport pandas as pd
```

Step 2: Set Up the URL to Scrape

We need to specify the URL of the website we want to scrape for links.

```python
url = "https://example.com" # Replace with the target URL
```

Step 3: Send an HTTP Request

We will use the Requests library to send an HTTP GET request to the specified URL.

```python
response = requests.get(url)

# Check if the request was successful if
response.status_code == 200:
print("Successfully fetched the webpage!")else:
print("Failed to retrieve the webpage. Status code:",
response.status_code)
```

Step 4: Parse the HTML Content

Now that we have the HTML response, we need to parse it
using Beautiful Soup.

```python
soup = BeautifulSoup(response.content, 'html.parser')
```

Step 5: Extract Links

Using Beautiful Soup, we can find all the links (`<a>`
tags) in the HTML. We'll extract the URLs from each link.

```python
links = []
for link in soup.find_all('a'):href = link.get('href')
if href:
links.append(href)
```

Step 6: Save Links to a DataFrame

To store our links neatly, we can use Pandas to create a

DataFrame.

```python
links_df = pd.DataFrame(links, columns=["Links"])

```

Step 7: Export to CSV

Finally, we can export the DataFrame to a CSV file for further analysis.

```python
links_df.to_csv("extracted_links.csv", index=False)
print("Links have been successfully saved to 'extracted_links.csv'.")
```

Complete Code

Here is a complete version of the web link scraper tool:

```python import requests
from bs4 import BeautifulSoupimport pandas as pd

def scrape_links(url):
# Send HTTP request and check response response = requests.get(url)
if response.status_code != 200:
print("Failed to retrieve the webpage. Status code:", response.status_code)return

# Parse HTML content
```

```python
soup = BeautifulSoup(response.content, 'html.parser')

# Extract linkslinks = []
for link in soup.find_all('a'):href = link.get('href')
if href:
links.append(href)

# Save links to DataFrame
links_df = pd.DataFrame(links, columns=["Links"])

# Export to CSV links_df.to_csv("extracted_links.csv",
index=False)
print("Links have been successfully saved to
'extracted_links.csv'.")

# Example usage
scrape_links("https://example.com") # Replace with the
target URL
```

Ethical Considerations

Before scraping any website, always remember to check the site's `robots.txt` file and its terms of service. This file indicates whether the site permits scraping and under what conditions. Always respect the guidelines set by webmasters, and avoid overloading servers with frequent requests.

Congratulations! You've successfully built a complete web link scraping tool. In this chapter, we explored the principles of web scraping, set up the necessary libraries, and crafted a functional tool to extract hyperlinks from a webpage. Remember that with great power comes great responsibility; always consider the ethical aspects of web scraping as you utilize this tool.

Designing and Structuring a Custom Web Scraping Script

Web scraping, the process of extracting data from web pages, can facilitate data analysis, competitive research, and content aggregation. However, crafting an effective web scraping script requires careful planning and structuring to ensure that it not only functions correctly but also adheres to legal and ethical standards. In this chapter, we will explore the essential components and best practices for designing and structuring a custom web scraping script.

Understanding the Basics of Web Scraping

Before diving into the design of a web scraping script, it is imperative to understand how web scraping works. At its core, web scraping involves sending an HTTP request to a server, retrieving the HTML response, and then parsing that HTML to extract useful information. This process can be broken down into several key components:

Making Requests: The first step in web scraping involves sending HTTP requests to the target website.

Libraries like `requests` in Python simplify this process.

Parsing HTML: Once the HTML content is retrieved, parsing tools such as Beautiful Soup or lxml can be used to navigate the HTML structure and extract the desired data.

Storing Data: After obtaining the relevant information, it's essential to store it in a structured format. This can be done using various methods, including saving to a CSV file, a database, or any other storage solution.

Respecting Robots.txt: Websites often provide a `robots.txt` file that dictates which parts of the site can be crawled. A responsible scraper must comply with these directives to avoid legal ramifications and maintain cordial relationships with website owners.

Rate Limiting: To avoid overwhelming a server with requests and possibly getting blocked, rate limiting is vital. This involves controlling the frequency of requests sent to the server.

Step 1: Defining Your Objectives

A successful web scraping project begins with a clear understanding of its objectives. Ask yourself the following questions:

What data am I trying to collect?
Why do I want this data, and how will I use it?
Which websites contain the data I need, and what are their structures?

Clearly defining these objectives will not only streamline the development process but will also guide the subsequent steps.

Step 2: Planning the Scraping Process

Once your objectives are set, it's time to plan the scraping process. This involves outlining the workflow and determining the necessary tools and technologies. Here's a proposed framework:

2.1 Identify Target Websites

Create a list of websites that contain the data you need. Analyze the HTML structure of these websites using the browser's developer tools to identify the elements containing the desired data.

2.2 Choose the Right Tools

Select a programming language that supports web scraping. Python is a popular choice due to its rich ecosystem of libraries.
Decide on libraries for making requests (e.g., `requests`), parsing HTML (e.g., Beautiful Soup, Scrapy), and storing data (e.g., SQLite, pandas).

2.3 Design the Data Flow

Define the flow of data starting from the request to the server, through parsing and finally to storage.
Consider edge cases, such as handling pagination and

dealing with dynamically loaded content (e.g.,JavaScript-rendered sites).

Step 3: Structuring the Script

With a clear plan in hand, it's time to structure your web scraping script. Below is a suggested outline: ### 3.1 Set Up the Environment
Begin by setting up your development environment, including installing necessary libraries.

```bash
pip install requests beautifulsoup4 pandas
```

3.2 Import Libraries

At the start of your script, import the required libraries.

```python
import requests
from bs4 import BeautifulSoup
import pandas as pd
```

3.3 Define Functions

Encapsulating logic into functions makes your script modular and easier to maintain. Typical functionsinclude:

fetch_page(url): Responsible for sending the HTTP request.
parse_html(html): Parses the HTML and extracts the required data.
store_data(data): Handles the storage of extracted

data.

```python
def fetch_page(url):
response = requests.get(url) response.raise_for_status()
return response.text

def parse_html(html):
soup = BeautifulSoup(html, 'html.parser')
# Example: Extracting titles from a webpage titles =
[title.text for title in soup.find_all('h1')]return titles

def store_data(data):
df      =      pd.DataFrame(data,      columns=['Title'])
df.to_csv('titles.csv', index=False)
```

3.4 Main Logic

The main logic of the script ties everything together, orchestrating the flow between fetching, parsing, and storing data.

```python
if __name__ == "__main__":
url = 'https://example.com'html = fetch_page(url) data =
parse_html(html) store_data(data)
```

Step 4: Testing and Debugging

Once your script is structured, thorough testing is crucial. Run the script on a small scale to verify itsfunctionality.

Watch for:

Errors: Handling exceptions gracefully to prevent crashes.
Data Accuracy: Ensuring the correct data is extracted.
Compliance: Verifying adherence to `robots.txt` and any legal requirements. ## Step 5: Maintenance and Adaptability
Websites frequently change their structures, and your script may need updates to keep functioning properly. Setting up a system for periodic checks, alerts for failures, and version control can enhance the longevity of your scraping efforts.

Designing and structuring a custom web scraping script is an intricate process that demands planning, attention to detail, and a respect for site policies. By clearly defining objectives, choosing the right tools, structuring the code effectively, and staying adaptable, you can create a powerful script that extracts valuable insights from the web. In an era of data-driven decision making, mastering web scraping can significantly enhance your analytical capabilities and provide a competitive edge.

Best Practices for Developing Scalable Web Link Scrapers

Web link scrapers are essential tools that automate the process of extracting data from websites. However, as the volume of data and the complexities of web structures increase, developing scalable web link scrapers becomes a challenge. This chapter outlines best practices to ensure that your web scrapers are efficient, maintainable, and capable of handling growing datasets over time.

1. Understand the Website Structure

Before diving into coding your web scraper, it's vital to understand the website's structure you intend to scrape. Familiarize yourself with the following:

HTML/CSS Structure: Use developer tools in browsers to inspect elements on the page and identify the tags that hold the data you're interested in.
JavaScript Rendering: Some websites use JavaScript frameworks to load content dynamically. Understand how the content is served, and consider using tools that support rendering JavaScript (e.g., Selenium, Puppeteer).
API Availability: Check if the website offers an API that provides the data you need in a structured manner. APIs are typically more stable and less resource-intensive to use than scraping.

2. Use a Modular Design

Design your scraper using a modular approach, which divides the application into separate components or modules. This allows:

Reusability: Components can be reused across different projects or scraping tasks.
Maintainability: If a bug is identified or functionality needs to change, you can update specific modules without affecting the entire application.
Ease of Testing: Smaller modules can be tested

independently, ensuring that each part of the scraper functions as expected.

Consider adopting a layered architecture, such as:

Data Extraction Layer: Responsible for retrieving HTML content.
Parsing Layer: Processes the HTML to extract useful data.
Storage Layer: Manages how extracted data is stored or written to a database.
Scheduling Layer: Handles the frequency and timing of scraping tasks. ## 3. Manage Concurrency and Rate Limiting
When scraping large volumes of data, managing concurrency and rate limiting is critical to avoid being blocked by the target website. Here are some strategies:

Throttling: Introduce delays between requests to avoid overwhelming the server. You can adjust the delay based on the target website's response time.
Concurrent Requests: Utilize libraries like `asyncio`, `aiohttp`, or `Scrapy` to manage multiple requests in parallel while still obeying rate limits.
Backoff Algorithms: Implement exponential backoff strategies to automatically wait longer periods between retries after encountering errors such as 429 Too Many Requests.

4. Handle Data Normalization and Storage Efficiently

When scraping large amounts of data, it's essential to normalize and store the data effectively:

Data Cleaning: Normalize data formats (e.g., dates, currencies) as you extract it to ensure consistency and ease of analysis.

Use Databases: Employ databases like PostgreSQL, MongoDB, or even cloud storage services to accommodate large datasets. Ensure that your database structure is designed to handle the data efficiently.

Batch Processing: Instead of storing data in real-time, consider batch processing, especially if you're dealing with high-frequency updates. This can improve performance and reduce database lock contention.

5. Implement Robust Error Handling

Inevitably, web scraping will encounter various issues, from network timeouts to changes in website structure. Implement robust error handling mechanisms that include:

Logging: Maintain logs for all scraping activities. This will help diagnostics when things go wrong.

Retry Logic: Establish logic to automatically retry requests that fail due to transient issues, while keeping an eye on the limits set by rate limiting guidelines.

Monitoring: Set up alerts for when scraping jobs fail or encounter significant changes in response codes.

6. Use a Headless Browser for Complex Sites

For websites that heavily rely on JavaScript or that employ anti-scraping measures, consider using a headless browser like Selenium or Puppeteer. These tools simulate a real user's interaction with the web page, enabling you to:

Interact with Dynamic Content: Extract content generated after page load, improving data completeness.
Emulate User Actions: Automate navigation, form submissions, and clicks.

However, be cautious about the higher resource utilization of headless browsers compared to traditional scrapers.

7. Respect Legal and Ethical Considerations

Always consider the legal and ethical implications of web scraping:

Terms of Service Compliance: Review the target website's terms of service to ensure that scraping is permitted. Some websites explicitly prohibit data scraping.
Robots.txt: Adhere to the guidelines set in the `robots.txt` file of the website, which specifies which parts of the site are open to crawlers.
Data Privacy: Be mindful of personal data and comply with regulations like GDPR. Avoid scraping personal information without consent.

8. Continuous Maintenance and Upgrading

The web is a dynamic environment, with constant changes made to websites. As such, scrapers require ongoing maintenance:

Monitor Change: Set up regular checks to ensure that the scraper continues to work as intended even as the target website updates its structure.
Upgrade Dependencies: Keep libraries and frameworks up-to-date to mitigate security vulnerabilities

and leverage new features.
User Feedback: If your scraper is part of a larger application, gather user feedback to understand pain points and areas for improvement.

Developing scalable web link scrapers requires a thoughtful approach that balances efficiency, legality, and maintainability. By following these best practices, not only will you create robust web scrapers that stand the test of time, but you'll also make your operations smoother, more efficient, and ready to handle the challenges of web data extraction in a rapidly evolving digital landscape. Remember, web scraping is both a technical skill and a responsible practice—approach it with care and ethical consideration.

Conclusion

In this book, we have journeyed through the intricate world of web scraping with Python, specifically focusing on the extraction of links from web pages. The skills and techniques discussed throughout have equipped you with the knowledge to navigate websites, collect relevant data, and build a foundation for more complex web scraping tasks.

We began our exploration by understanding the fundamental concepts of web scraping, emphasizing the importance of ethical practices, compliance with terms of service, and the legal considerations involved. By establishing a solid groundwork, we prepared you to approach web scraping not just as a technical skill, but as a responsible practice.

As we delved deeper, we covered essential libraries such as Beautiful Soup and Scrapy, providing you with hands-on examples and practical applications. You learned how to parse HTML, navigate the Document Object Model (DOM), and adeptly handle different web structures. The exercises and code snippets were designed to foster your coding proficiency and give you the confidence to tackle real-world web scraping challenges.

Moreover, we highlighted the potential obstacles you might encounter, such as anti-scraping measures and dynamic content generated by JavaScript. You were guided on various strategies to overcome these hurdles, empowering you to be adaptable and resourceful in your scraping endeavors.

As you close this book, take a moment to reflect on what you've learned. The ability to scrape links from the web opens up a wealth of opportunities for research, data analysis, and even personal projects that can enhance your understanding of a particular domain. Remember that the world of data is vast and ever-changing, and your skills in Python web scraping can serve as a powerful tool to access and leverage that information.

As you move forward, we encourage you to experiment with different websites and projects, to continuouslyrefine your scraping techniques, and to stay abreast of the evolving landscape of web technologies. The possibilities are limitless, and with persistence and curiosity, you can unveil the treasures hidden within the web.

Thank you for joining us on this adventure into Python scraping. We hope you feel inspired and empowered to explore the digital world around you, and we wish you the best in your future scraping endeavors. Happycoding!

Biography

Alex Hart is a passionate tech enthusiast and the creative mind behind numerous books, including the highly-anticipated *Hart*. With a rich background in **cybersecurity, web development, and Python programming**, Alex brings a unique blend of skills to the digital world.

His expertise extends to **ethical hacking and web scraping**, where he has spent years mastering the art of gathering and securing data online. As a true tech wizard, Alex has a knack for breaking down complex concepts into accessible insights for readers eager to dive into the world of code and cybersecurity.

Beyond his professional pursuits, Alex is a lifelong learner and a hacker at heart—always tinkering with the latest tools and technologies to push the boundaries of what's possible. When he's not behind a computer screen, Alex enjoys exploring **cutting-edge cybersecurity trends** and developing new ways to make the web a safer place.

Driven by a deep passion for technology and an unstoppable curiosity, Alex Hart's books offer both practical knowledge and a glimpse into the exciting, fast-paced world of coding and cyber defense. Whether you're a seasoned developer or just starting your journey, Alex's work will inspire you to think critically, code smartly, and stay ahead of the curve.

Glossary: Python Scrape for Links in Web

1. Web Scraping

Definition: Web scraping is an automated method used to extract large amounts of data from websites. It often involves fetching a web page's content and parsing the information to retrieve specific data points.

2. Hyperlink

Definition: A hyperlink (or link) is a reference to a document or resource that users can click to navigate to another location on the web. In HTML, hyperlinks are created using the `<a>` (anchor) tag.

3. Python

Definition: Python is a high-level programming

language known for its readability and versatility. It is widely used in web scraping due to its vast collection of libraries and frameworks.

4. HTML (HyperText Markup Language)

Definition: HTML is the standard markup language used to create web pages. It structures the content on the page and defines elements such as headings, paragraphs, images, and links.

5. Library

Definition: In programming, a library is a collection of pre-written code that developers can use to perform specific tasks without having to write the code from scratch. For web scraping in Python, popular libraries include Requests, Beautiful Soup, and Scrapy.

6. Requests

Definition: Requests is a Python library used to make HTTP requests easier. It allows you to send GET and POST requests to retrieve the contents of web pages.

7. Beautiful Soup

Definition: Beautiful Soup is a Python library designed for parsing HTML and XML documents. It provides Pythonic idioms for iterating, searching, and modifying the parse tree, making it easier to extract data from HTML tags.

8. Scrapy

Definition: Scrapy is an open-source web crawling framework for Python. It provides tools and features for building web scrapers efficiently and is particularly useful for scraping large volumes of data.

9. CSS Selector

Definition: A CSS selector is a pattern used to select the elements you want to style in your HTML document. In web scraping, CSS selectors can be used in libraries like Beautiful Soup to identify specific tags or attributes in HTML.

10. XPath

Definition: XPath is a language used for navigating through elements and attributes in XML and HTML documents. It can be used for more complex data extraction tasks in web scraping.

11. Data Cleaning

Definition: Data cleaning refers to the process of preparing and transforming raw data into a usable format. This often involves removing duplicates, correcting errors, and standardizing formats.

12. API (Application Programming Interface)

Definition: An API is a set of rules and protocols for building and interacting with software applications. Many websites provide APIs that you can use to access their data in a structured format, often eliminating the need to scrape HTML.

13. User-Agent

Definition: A User-Agent is a string that a web browser sends to a web server to identify itself. When scraping, it's common to set a User-Agent in the HTTP request to mimic a real browser and avoid being blocked by the website.

14. Rate Limiting

Definition: Rate limiting is a technique used by websites to control the amount of requests a user can make in a given time frame. When scraping, it's important to respect these limits to avoid getting blocked.

15. Robots.txt

Definition: The `robots.txt` file is a standard used by websites to communicate with web crawlers and bots about which pages they are allowed to access or scrape. Respecting these directives is essential for ethical web scraping.

www.ingramcontent.com/pod-product-compliance
Lightning Source LLC
LaVergne TN
LVHW051327050326
832903LV00031B/3412